EVAngelize

A Guide to Developing Your Evangelistic Ministry

Apostle, Dr. Terika Smith

TSM Publishing
530 Broadway, 3rd FL
Lawrence, Massachusetts 01841

Apostle, Dr. Terika Smith

Copyright © 2020 by Dr. Terika T. Smith/Terika Smith Ministries

All rights reserved. No part of this book may be reproduced in any form without the permission in writing from the publisher, except in the case of brief quotations embodied in critical articles or reviews.

All scripture quotation unless otherwise indicated are taken from The Holy Bible, New Living Translation1996 and King James Version, 1960. Used by permission. All rights reserved.

Designed by RichWired
Author's Photo: Gavino Photography

Manufactured in the United States of America
For any ordering information or special discounts for bulk purchases, please contact us @ terika5021@gmail.com

Published in the United States by TSM Publishing
ISBN # 978-0-9965967-5-6

Apostle, Dr. Terika Smith

TABLE OF CONTENTS

FOREWORD 1

WITH GRATITUDE 3

ABOUT THE BOOK 7

WHO IS THIS BOOK FOR? 11

WHY I HAD TO WRITE THIS BOOK 13

YOUR MINISTRY IS ABOUT TO SHIFT 17

INTRODUCTION 1

HOW TO USE THIS BOOK MOVING FORWARD? 23

CHAPTER 1 25

FRESH WIND TO EVANGELISM 25

CHAPTER 2 33

CHAPTER 3 42

CHAPTER 4 66

CHAPTER 5 82

CHAPTER 6 100

CHAPTER 7	104
CONCLUSION	107
ABOUT THE AUTHOR	112
OTHER BOOKS BY DR. TERIKA SMITH	115
NOTES	116

Foreword

There are some people you remember due to events, some through family business ties, others through other attachments or their profession. I remember Dr. Terika Smith due to all the above in addition to her being our daughter and colleague in Ministry.

As a Pentecostal Minister of the Church of God, I have read and actually implemented quite a number of writings on Evangelism. I find that each writer tends to piggy-back on other writers' ideas in order to improve their work. Having read the EVAngelize Book and I am convinced that this is one of the most practical and user-friendly applications I have seen to date.

We are living in a time when communication has risen to heights not seen before and the methods used yesteryear, though they have their place, they are not as practical today. In obedience to "The Great Commission" (Matt.28), we are to use any and every tool at our disposal to bring people to Christ, and the EVAngelize Plan is the most practical I have seen to date. It is thoughtful and easy to follow.

Apostle, Dr. Terika T. Smith is a transformed writer whose background is in education. I have watched her evolved over the years from an athlete, to a teacher, Principal, Pastor, Apostle and writer of numerous publications. At the time of this writing Dr. Smith is completing her fourth book.

In my opinion the EVAngelize Plan is The how-to on evangelism and deserves a spot in the hand of every serious Christian.

Bishop G Smith
State Senior Coordinator

With Gratitude

This book is dedicated to the loves of my life. I am blessed that so many special people fall into that category. Here is the shortlist.

First, I especially want to thank my parents, Bishop George and Rev. Evadney Smith. They have been a tremendous encouragement and inspiration in my life – not just as parents but because of who they are – their consistency and persona. They fear God above all. Loving, giving, encouraging, relentless, persevering, and the list truly goes on. They are second to none. The way they raised the four of us after migrating from Jamaica, leaving everything to go to a country they did not know. The way they sacrificed, at times working three jobs each while all six were in school at the same time. The way they challenged us, regardless our age to never quit, never give up, and to always have a plan. My parents are dreamers and they inspire us to also be dreamers. It's not okay to just be, there is always more.

Second, this book is dedicated to my siblings, including my in-laws: Karen Miclausi, Morvin and Diane Smith (Kurtis) and Dwight and Janis Smith. I am thankful to each of my siblings for their inspiration to strive for more, to never settle. We have all gleaned from the example of our parents and made conscious decisions to move forward. We all have our own families and professions, with the foundation that our parents taught us of Christ in the center and daring us to be dreamers. We have all grown and gone in different directions, yet we are anchored in the truth of our foundation.

It is reassuring to know that regardless of where I am in this world, should I scrape a knee and my siblings learn of it, immediately my phone would be ringing or the doorbell. Thank you, guys, for being part of my inspiration. I am equally thankful for their spouses, my in-laws. Each has encouraged me to persevere; each has shown me support with the same love as though we were all from the same parents. Thank you

This book is dedicated to my nephews and nieces: Omar Wisdom, Yesica Wisdom, Daniel Miclausi, Justin Smith, Jaqui Smith, Jordan Smith, Sierra Smith, Dwight Smith Jr. From changing diapers to watching you now as adults, living your lives and in many ways following the same foundation established not only by your parents but grandparents also. The tenacity of mom and dad reflect the tenacity of grandma and granddaddy. I encourage you guys, "Don't stop dreaming. Don't stop striving to do and be the best at what you do." I love you guys.

Lastly, God has blessed me with a daughter and son-in-law who, combined have given me three wonderful grandchildren: Ava, Gavin and Lia. This book along with all my other work, I dedicate to my daughter, – my "mama," my "nutcracker," my "little lady," Karen Andujar. From the moment God gave me you to parent, I have loved you and felt even more inspired to become the best God has called me to be. I knew you were watching, and I would tell the Lord, I wanted to be just like Him because you were watching. You continue to be a HUGE inspiration for me in writing books and doing what I do. I love you mama.

A special thank you as well to my church family, Flowing Rivers International Church for being such a tower of strength for me. Thank you for your wisdom and support.

Then Jesus came to them and said, 'All authority in heaven and on earth has been given to me. Therefore, go and make disciples of all nations, baptizing them in the name of the Father and of the Son and of the Holy Spirit, and teaching then to obey everything I have commanded you. And surely I am with you always, to the very end of the age.'"

Mathew 28:18-20 (KJV)

About The Book

The book EVAngelize is designed for any ministry that is looking for a fresh approach to evangelism. Too often we pick up a manual or visit a program, all of which are good and return home inspired to make a difference within our community and then nothing happens. Too often we invite men and women of God to spend time in workshops with our ministry teams, training them in the art of evangelism and then the speaker leaves, and implementation is minimal, if any. The goal here is not to look at what is wrong and make unhealthy statements regarding the integrity of one program from the other. Everything has its time, place and effectiveness according to the need of the community.

When considering writing this book, what came to mind was my own ministry and others like mine who are young in terms of years of existence and needing a fresh approach from what we grew up seeing. How do we engage our church community with the world around us? Are we still in the age of handing out tracks? Do they still even work? How do we capture the attention of our current society that has so many options from which to choose? These are tough questions and do not have a one size fits all approach answer.

EVAngelize

EVAngelize is a book that considers three points that I believe to be key in at least initiating the dialogue around community soul winning. The book is interactive and will engage you, the reader to consider your own ministry and ways to add to or continue what you are currently doing.

In this book you will guide your ministry development around the EVA of Evangelism:

1. Establish a plan
2. Know your Vicinity
3. Walk in your Authority

Who Is This Book For?

"Then Jesus came to them and said, 'All authority in heaven and on earth has been given to me. Therefore, go and make disciples of all nations, baptizing them in the name of the Father and of the Son and of the Holy Spirit, and teaching then to obey everything I have commanded you. And surely I am with you always, to the very end of the age.'"
Mathew 28:18-20 (KJV)

The text is clear on the mandate of the great commission of Christ for ALL nations. There is no partiality in who the church is to become a ministry to. Anyone who has a heart for Christ and a desire to win souls for the kingdom of God is invited to journey through this book with me. This book is for ministries looking to do the following things:

- Win the community for Christ
- Minister to young people
- Minister to adults
- Minister to addicts
- Minister to prostitutes
- Minister to professionals
- Minister to the uneducated or undereducated
- Minster to businessmen and women
- Minister to ALL nations

EVAngelize

Basically, if you are alive, and want to be a good steward of your time and have NO idea where to begin and how to do it, this book is for YOU!

I know this book will help your ministry in developing the three key areas of evangelism, the EVA of evangelism:

1. Establish a plan
2. Know your Vicinity
3. Walk in your Authority

Why I HAD To Write This Book

I am often invited to speak and train leaders. In my other life as an educator, I wrote and lead training sessions ranging from curriculum development, leadership development, instructional best practices and building team competencies. This is the short end of the list of courses, but I thought I would mention a few. Now that I am in ministry, I see a GREAT need to share my skills of bringing out the best in people. I am not tooting my own horn, but I love and have always loved seeing the potential realized in people and doing my best to bring it out of them. Why should this be any different?

The book EVAngelize is my opportunity to bring a practical approach to ministry on our mandate of the Great Commission, making the process more tangible than it is now. Additionally, I see so many small churches that are starting up, some with God given mandates and some with the mandate of, "This is not working, let's gather and start our own." Don't misunderstand, this is not to say God is not in the latter but rather that the starting of a church IS a delicate matter and MUST be entered with careful prayer and direction from God.

EVAngelize

We are living in a day with too many pulpit homicides, too many men and women taking their lives while preaching to others the blessing of living a God-fearing life. There are too many churches looking for THE answer when really the answer does not need to be looked for, it was never lost. God is present and patient. The love of God is as real today as it was yesterday; it was never lost; we just need to have our eyes open to find it. We don't need to open more buildings; we need to open more hearts, beginning with our own. Can I get an AMEN?

EVAngelize takes us back to our first love and the why it is a blessing and a privilege to serve the Lord. It is a reminder that God's love is not a denomination nor a title but who we are to be as believers. If we go back to the reason as to why we serve God, we should find that it was because we had an encounter with His love. If that is not the case, this book might not be for you. You cannot evangelize by sharing a message you do not participate in.

Apostle, Dr. Terika Smith

Your Ministry is About to Shift

This book will provoke you to take a deeper look at your ministry and what you are or are not doing to win souls for the kingdom. If you as a pastor or leader are transparent about your methodology, you might find that a lot of what you are currently doing could be more effective with just a few adjustments. Or, you might find that your ministry is new, or you have not yet employed an evangelistic ministry approach. That's okay. When our church started, our focus was NOT on evangelism. God put it on my heart to take the first few years to teach the word of God, and to pour into the ministry from every possible angle, the living word of God. From there, I have seen us develop a strong leadership base, which is now ready to tackle the multitude God is sending.

I had an aha moment some years ago when I read the scripture, "The harvest is ripe but the laborers are few, pray to the Lord of the harvest that He might send workers…" I can't tell you how many times I heard pastors and leaders pray for souls to come to church. I know I made that mistake countless times. Don't get me wrong, I am not saying you should never pray for souls. However, if the world is already full of souls, why pray for what is in abundance? The word of God says to pray for workers, pray to one who oversees the workers to send more workers. What do you do as a pastor when you get an addict in your church and you do not have a worker that can relate with him or her? What do you do when you get a prostitute in your church?

EVAngelize

Do you have a worker that can work with him or her?

This book has the goal of really provoking thought that will prayerfully shift your ministry and your attitude towards evangelism. There are a lot of souls out there, let us not let them die without coming to know Christ as their Lord and Savior.

INTRODUCTION

What is Evangelism?

"Then Jesus came to them and said, 'All authority in heaven and on earth has been given to me. Therefore, go and make disciples of all nations, baptizing them in the name of the Father and of the Son and of the Holy Spirit, and teaching them to obey everything I have commanded you. And surely I am with you always, to the very end of the age.'"
Mathew 28:18-20 (KJV)

The Great Commission

I preached a sermon once about the mission of commission. What the Lord placed in my spirit at the time was the importance of understanding the mission. What was the task at hand that we needed to lay focus on in order to fulfill the roles and responsibilities we have been assigned? When we think of a mission statement for example, it is the execution plan of the vision that guides the direction of an entity, be it individual or organization. The word of God says,

Where there is no vision, the people perish.
Proverbs 29:18 KJV

I take it a step further by saying, not only where there is no vision the people will perish, but where there are people with vision but no mission there is no direction.

The simple revelation I received was that direction is birthed out of a seed that is planted into the sight, insight or foresight of the one who is leading. So then, the mission is the plan or blueprint necessary to guide the vision into action. Let's consider the obvious, if something is planted, then there is a planter. If a seed is planted, then there is ground to receive it. Ground cannot produce what has not been planted. The seed could not have grown in the ground, had there not been a planter to put the seed there in the first place. A vision is a seed that comes from the heart of the planter into ground that is ready to receive and reproduce. The time between the planting and the reproduction takes time, intentional time, where germination, revelation and expansion will take place. If we can hold on to that analogy, let us consider the mission of commission. It is impossible to effectively commission someone to move forward on a mission unless they have been fully indoctrinated. What was planted into them? What does it look like? And how is it incorporated into their daily walk? Each step of the way we are seeing germination, revelation, and expansion.

According to Merriam Webster Dictionary, several definitions of commission are as follows:

- 1a: a formal written warrant granting the power to perform various acts or duties
- 2a: an authorization or command to act in a prescribed manner or to perform prescribed acts: CHARGE
- 3a: authority to act for, in behalf of, or in place of another

There is a transaction enforce. There is the delegation of power granted to someone to act on behalf of another. We must be certain that, that is not an overnight experience but rather a carefully executed transaction that is the result of a relationship developed over time. Additionally, there is trust that the recipient will work in agreement with the one who made the commission to execute the plan at hand without modification to suit their own needs. If apple seeds are planted, the fruit it MUST bear is apples, not oranges. My working definition of the word commission in this book is as follows:

Collaboration coupled with participation of the recipient of the mission, with the mission.

True collaboration takes place the moment the mission shifts from an individual into teamwork. The one issuing the mission now is in collaboration with the one who receives it in their hands.

If we look at the context of the text of Mathew 28:18-20, we see where Jesus is speaking with the disciples. He begins by sharing what had been given to him. Now note this, the disciples had been with Jesus for a little over three years. They had seen Jesus in action, teaching multitudes, healing the sick, raising the dead, casting out demons, multiplying fish and bread, rebuking the elements and more. They too participated in performing some of these signs as he commissioned them while he walked with them…… One might say, "Wait, didn't he already have ALL authority?" Well the answer is though he was God, He subjected himself to the law of the land - this is such a deep subject, but let's explore it briefly - He performed the works of the Spirit while He walked the earth in the form of man to fulfil the plan of His father. He constantly stated that His will was to do His father's will. You see, He too was commissioned. Jesus was on a mission to participate in the commission of His father. He could not deviate from the plan. He could not integrate His own agenda. He had to fully collaborate with the mission to restore man to his original intent. Man was intended to have dominion and subdue the land. Sin and death were not intended to dominate humanity. They were not intended to enter in and remove intimacy between the planter and the earth He put the seed of life into.

When Jesus said to His disciples, ALL authority is given to Him in heaven and on earth, it was a statement of restored governance. He was literally telling them, what He had before was limited to one dimension, however, what He had now, because of His obedience to the complete execution of the mission He was commissioned to do has propelled Him to a level of total authority. His authority span was now in heaven, on earth and if we move a step further in understanding scripture, to under the earth. His conquest of death, hell and the grave gave Him authority over the house of the strongman, which is Satan. So, ALL authority now belongs to Jesus. With that authority, He now commissions us all to walk as He walked, speak as He spoke and act as He acted.

There are five parts to the Great Commission:
- Go
- Make
- Baptize
- Teach
- Model

In a summarized text of three verses, Jesus lays out the blueprint to the mission of conquering the world for the sake of the Gospel. Each step is interconnected with the other. None of these can work in isolation, each needs the other. Let me explain.

Point 1- Go

The only way for a person to "go" is if they rise from where they are and step into action. Regardless of how great or small, movement is required for the execution of any plan to take place. Jesus told the disciples to go into ALL the world. Whether walking, running, on a camel a horse, a bike, a plane, or whatever the transportation method one might use, movement is required to reach the destination.

A vision has a mark or a destination. There must be a goal to be achieved for the recipient of the vision to begin the journey. God told Abram, "Go to a land I will show you." Jesus told his disciples, "Go into all the world." He did not put a name, a nation or a language. He said, "Go into ALL the world." Here, we are considering world to not be exclusive to traveling to faraway lands but also the diverse ethnicities around us. Jesus was saying go to all ages, all races, all languages, all cultures, all creeds, all social classes, ALL. It was never Jesus' intention that there be so much division in churches, denominations, and cultural groups. So, He told them "Go, get up and go."

Point 2 – Make

When you make something, there is a model, an ingredient and a methodology in order to get the product made. There are steps that are intentionally designed to yield the outcome of the intended product. Jesus just told them He had all authority and power. He just told them to go everywhere and make a product, disciples. Jesus is speaking to His disciples as a teacher speaks to their students. I have taught you all that you will need to pour into others the way I poured into you. In the book of John Ch.14, Jesus went as far as to tell them that all that He, Jesus did, they could do as well. He also told them that they would be able to do greater works than Him. It was not that they or we are greater than Jesus, never. Jesus was saying to them as He also speaks to us, "The hard part is over, I have paved the way, EVERYTHING that can hinder your movement has been defeated. There are more of you than the one off me, so go out and imitate what I did. Pour into people like I poured into you. Correct them as I corrected you. Instruct them as I instructed you. Hold them accountable as I held you accountable. Stretch their faith as I stretched your faith. Teach them to heal as I healed, deliver as I delivered, restore as I restored. Everything I put in you, take the time to put into them. Do it one step at a time."

Consider the concept of "make" as in taking the skills and personalities of people who are like you into consideration when making them disciples. If you have educated people, their approach to learning may be different from individuals who are not as educated. In like fashion, you can have doctors and lawyers in a room but if the lesson is exclusively about medicine, the lawyers may all get lost or lose interest. Why is this so important? Make requires discernment and active spiritual participation on the side of the teacher to ensure that what they are depositing in those they are discipling will bring out the best of the anointing that is in them. I put it this way for the ministry I lead and suggest the same for your as well. As we follow the model that Jesus laid out for us, let us not try to imitate an awesome plan that served one ministry. It was awesome for that time and that season. However, you have a unique anointing over yourself, your ministry and anything God puts in your hand. The disciples "you" make will all fall in accordance with the anointing that is over your life and ministry. The Holy Spirit will give you the language to make communication and collaboration meaningful.

Point 3 – Baptize

The word baptize comes from the Greek word baptizo meaning to submerge. In order to submerge something, there is a hand of authority that is holding fast onto the thing it is submerging, in this case, a person. The one doing the submerging MUST be one with greater authority to the one being submerged. When John The Baptist baptized Jesus, he was on the land at the time; in greater authority than Jesus. John The Baptist was the one the prophets spoke about in the book of Isaiah 40, the one crying in the wilderness, paving the way for the Lord.

John was preaching for the people to repent of their sins and be baptized in water. He would go on to tell the people that someone greater than he was coming. This person would baptize with Holy Ghost and fire (Matthew 3:11). This person, John would say would be the deliverer of all mankind. Jesus, who knew no sin, came to John so that He could be baptized with the expressed purpose of crucifying the flesh, fulfilling the will of God and being positioned for service. It was at this point that Jesus' ministry was launched on the land.

Baptism for the church is that outward declaration that one is willing to die to self and live a surrendered life to the will of God. This is exactly what Jesus did and so should we.

Point 4 – Teach

I find it interesting, don't you, that Jesus told the disciples to go, make, baptize and then take time to teach? As ministry shifted in my life and I began to look more closely at God's word and as I lead his people, I noticed that the difference between these two words have become more meaningful. When you are teaching something, you are causing others to come into knowledge or understanding of what you know or the information you are covering.

Teaching requires more skills than making. You can make something without teaching the why and how of the correct ingredients, like following the pictures on the box. When you teach a person how to make something, the logic behind the process, and how to get excellent results, they no longer need the picture on the box to be successful. An excellent chef does not need a box, they need skills, tools and ingredients. An excellent instructor does not teach text, they know how to make learning meaningful regardless the learning capacity of each learner before them.

Jesus had disciples from different walks of life. He told them to teach the new disciples all they had learned from Him. In other words, take the time to pour into the new disciples until they were ready for commissioning. I can hear Jesus saying, "When you teach, teach them so they can go further than you can go. Just like I taught you to go further than I went"

Point 5 – Model (Me)

Jesus was specific, He told them, "Teaching them to obey everything I taught you…" He didn't say, "What you thought you learned or what you liked about the lesson." He didn't say, "Teach them parts that come easy to you." A disciple pays close attention to everything their teacher/leader does, giving close attention to the details. The only way to do a thing like your leader does is to become like him or her. Jesus was careful not to just dismiss them. He told them, "Do it like I did it, MODEL ME. Become like Me so all can see Me in you."

Within the fabric of the Great Commission is evangelism and the evangelist within us. Some might say, "I was not born to be an evangelist or that is not my calling." While your calling might not be to travel and expound the Word of God like a Jimmy Swaggart or John Wesley, every person who's life has been touched by God, has a message for someone who is currently wearing the shoes they once wore.

Evangelism

The word evangelism simply means to spread or preach the gospel. Note, the word preach does not denote you need a pulpit. It means you have the heart to open your mouth and release a word that will change lives. Evolving from the word Evangel for the gospels, we can agree that this is relating to the releasing of the Gospel of Jesus Christ as you open your mouth. Paul tells us, about evangelism, that we need two things, people and a product. We need people who are willing to go and when they go, there must be a product that they carry with them. He also makes it clear that, 'people go when they are sent.'

14 How, then, can they call on the one they have not believed in? And how can they believe in the one of whom they have not heard? And how can they hear without someone preaching to them? 15 And how can anyone preach unless they are sent? As it is written: "How beautiful are the feet of those who bring good news!"] 16 But not all the Israelites accepted the good news. For Isaiah says, "Lord, who has believed our message?" 17 Consequently, faith comes from hearing the message, and the message is heard through the word about Christ.
Romans 10:14-17, NIV

Based on the goal of this book, we will look at evangelism as requiring a plan and a process in place. I believe every ministry needs to at some point sit and consider what it is doing in the spirit of evangelism and consider their level of effectiveness. CAUTION, your measure is NOT based on the church down the street. It is based on the Word of God and the vision God deposited into the ground of the ministry's leadership. This is very important. If you, as an individual or church develop an imitator spirit, or try to be like the joneses down the street, you will grow to the capacity of the Joneses, and not to the capacity that God intended for you to grow.

Always keep in mind, there are many forms of resources, tools that you can use as you build your ministry, some of which have yet to be built. These steps are suggestions that I value and employ in my ministry and ministries who seek out our support.

Three must haves:

- Have a plan. Before embarking on evangelism or any ministry, take time to plan, you will thank me later.
    o What is the plan?
    ☐ Is it a long term or short-term plan?
    ☐ Does this plan align with the vision of the church?
    ☐ If you are not the pastor, is your pastor on board with the plan?
    o Where will you begin or release your ministry for evangelism?

- Why is it important to you as an individual?
- Why is it important to your ministry?
- How will it impact your ministry directly or indirectly?
- How will it impact your leadership?
- How will it impact the supports you currently provide?

- Have a team. People will act if there is leadership equipped to lead them. This is a trust issue, yes, even in ministry.

  - Establish a team that has a passion for souls, support of leadership, and vision for church growth and expansion. The team can do two things, more as God leads you.

- Determine when it requires a whole church evangelism.
- Determine when it is a ministry specific evangelism
- Have a pattern for all to follow, this is your means to an end
- Establish a pattern that makes sense for your congregation
- Establish a pattern that complements the community you are serving and make it adaptable as you grow
- Make sure your pattern is transferable from children's ministry, to men's ministry, to adult ministry. and so on.

As stated before, and I will continue to reiterate throughout this text, these are suggestions, this process on how to move your ministry serves as a guide for you and your ministry. Later we will look closely at the EVA of EVAngelism. Regardless of the type of ministry you have, you need a working understanding around evangelism and the necessary steps on how to build your team and grow your church.

Next we will take a look at two types of evangelists, those who look and sound like you and I as we share the gospel in our homes, on the streets, on the job, etc. Then there are the evangelists who have an anointing to lead mass crusades, millions of people coming to Christ in one gathering.

Evangelist

The largest recorded evangelistic crusade of the disciples was in Acts chapter 2 following the baptism of the Holy Spirit. The Disciples were baptized in the Holy Spirit and everyone thought they were drunk at 9am. Peter stood up and under the anointing of the Holy Spirit, preached his first sermon. He ministered to everyone there and over 3 thousand were added to the church on that first day. Men and women confessing Jesus Christ as Lord. Peter brought the good news of the Gospel to all who were there.

An evangelist is a bringer of good tidings. In other words, he brings good news. Evangelism has been stated as the spreading of The Good News, the Word of Jesus Christ. The charge of the evangelist is to ensure that wherever they go, they are the vessels used for the conveying of the Gospel. The Apostle Paul in 2 Timothy 4:5, "But you, keep your head in all situations, endure hardship, do the work of an evangelist, discharge all the duties of your ministry." His message was manifold, telling Timothy to do four key things in the spirit of maintaining the integrity of the call:

•	Keep his head above all situations or stay clear of whatever may drown his thinking and rob him of his focus to the call to ministry on his life

•	Endure hardship which is a guaranteed path of all who serve the Lord. We must remember, as Christ suffered so will those who are called by Him. We remember Jesus told Cornelius in the book of Acts of the Apostles that Paul would learn to suffer for the gospel.

•	The evangelist is constantly in the field, so it is important that they remember that there are certain situations that might get them distracted (situations we bring on ourselves) and it's not the enemy. Having an eye of discernment is key.

•	Do the work of an evangelist, one with a constant word that brought salvation through the conviction of the Holy Spirit, paying close attention to not contaminate the word of God with personal agendas.

o   I want us to keep in mind that the call to spread the Gospel was a command that was given to all people; everyone has a hand in doing the work of an evangelist. Not just those who are evangelists leading great crusades. No matter what your calling is or what God has placed for you to do, you should still "do the work of an evangelist.

- Discharge all the duties of His ministry, in other words, the evangelist has a divine responsibility upon entering a town to bring transformation to the minds and hearts of the hearers. To preach with authority the infallible word of God:

o   Bringing salvation to the lost
o   Casting out demons
o   Healing the sick
o   Delivering the oppressed

It is my belief in accordance with scripture, primarily the text used at the beginning of this chapter, and the base of this book, that the Great Commission is meant for ALL who believe. Therefore, there is an evangelist in all of us. Everyone has a testimony to share that could change the life of another towards living a life surrendered to Christ. I also believe that there are men and women, who are specifically called for this purpose. Ephesians 4:11 states, *"So Christ himself gave the apostles, the prophets, the evangelists, the pastors and teachers."*

The Word of God highlights here that Jesus Christ, the commissioner of us all, released an anointing upon the church to function in different capacities. This does not preclude a person from functioning in multiple capacities, it simply is telling us that there is a calling and a responsibility associated to each person called with their respective anointing. To further explain, I can be an evangelist and teach.

Teaching may not be my gifting but when called upon, with the right material before me, I can deliver a lesson before a small intimate group of people. Does that make me a teacher, no, it means I am surrendered to God using me in the capacity He wants when there is a need.

On the day of Pentecost, the release of the Holy Spirit was the release of the fivefold anointing upon all flesh. We should note that this ONE Holy Spirit is the ONE who anointed all. This ONE came out of ONE man, Jesus Christ. That being said, my revelation to the text is that within Jesus Christ were all 5 folds; the Apostle, Prophet, Evangelist, Pastor, and Teacher. Throughout scripture and even in our day, we see men and women of God used in multiple capacities, however, there is always an area of strength that really marks the person. I love what I do. God has used me to prophecy, I am an ordained pastor and apostle, and I teach.

I have also led evangelistic services in Latin America and Africa. I have been told and I do agree, that there is a spark that overtakes me when I am teaching. I LOVE to teach. I love breaking down the text. I am sharing my personal testimony here because I do not want anyone thinking to themselves, "I have to choose" or "what am I good for?" Find your passion and chase after it, God has already gifted you in your passion sphere.

The evangelist is one of those gifting spheres. You notice, you love the local congregation, yet you are drawn to the streets, other communities, and parts of the world. This is not, however, a license to take off and do what you want. The evangelist MUST understand that they are under authority as Jesus was under authority. It is important to get the blessing of their Pastor, Apostle, or Bishop. The figure to whom they report, get fed by, and are mentored. Yes, the Evangelist is one of the gifts given by Jesus to the Church, but we must remember, all come from ONE Holy Spirit and He comes from the Father, through Jesus Christ the Son to us the church. To run off and do what one wants because of a title or they "felt" led to is out of divine order. It is done today, but that does not make it right.

Please note, I have distinguished between the evangelist that is in all of us. We are all called to evangelize. However, there are those who that gifting sphere is who they are, when you think of the Jimmy Swaggart who lead so many crusades over his lifetime, you think Evangelist. He has done so much for the kingdom but what he has been noted for has been his evangelistic crusades.

So, what are you? Are you a part of the body of evangelists which is all of us? Or, are you called by God to be an Evangelist to the world? Tough to answer but look at your fruits and you will know the answer.

Evangelism Do's and Don'ts

In this short section, I thought I should share some short do's and don'ts about evangelism. I am sure you might have a longer or shorter list. This list comes from teachings I have done in my own church during Sunday Bible studies.

- You do not need a plane, train, or automobile to begin a ministry of evangelism, it starts at home. Let home be the first place you evangelize, then spread out into your local community, if they reject you, do not stop, go to the next. Your passion for souls will lead you to the doors that are already open and waiting for your arrival.

- It's not about you. Do not try to evangelize, placing full emphasis on yourself and what you do. The purpose of evangelism is to engage the person about the love of Christ so focus on Him and His love.

- Allow yourself to be 100% lead by the Holy Spirit. When you do this, the Holy Spirit leads you into terrain that has already been prepared for you. He will give you the words, He will respond to your prayers not because it is what you want but because in Him sending you there you would be fulfilling the will of God. When He takes you to a house of addicts, He has already given you the terrain. In fact, the principalities over that house see you from a far and will try to prevent you from entering because they know their hold on that territory has come to an end. Let HIM lead.

- Remember, when you go out to evangelize, do not look for it to become a preaching opportunity. I go back to; this is not about you. Let the Holy Spirit lead. Testify when you must, share the scripture He puts in your spirit and wait for His instructions. When you pray, let HIM pray through you. Do not begin shouting like you are in a pulpit. The biggest and best Bible you can carry is the one in your heart.

- You will have a lasting impact when you can share what God has done in your life

    o   In under a minute, share what it was
    - Where were you?
    - What was it?
    - How did it happen?
    - How can they too be blessed?

- **REMEMBER**: The testimony you share each time will vary based on the WHY God has sent you to an area. Be ready for God to use you.
  - How can it happen for them?
  - Invite them to prayer
  - Lead them into the plan of salvation
  - Close with a prayer of blessing for closure

- KISS Method
  - Keep
  - It
  - Simple
  - Sweetie

  - **NOTE**: No one is stupid, which is why I opted to use the word sweetie. The idea here is that in all that you do, your time and the time of the ones you are ministering to is precious. You will get more in and more out if you keep your time together simple. The longer you go the more you overstay your welcome. When you stay too long, consider what implications that can have of the newly formed relationship that is still digesting what they just received. A spirit of codependency can begin when someone sees in you what they do not have or need and latch on in a way that may not be healthy to either parties. It important to emphasize at times to people you minister to that you are an evangelist not their pastor. A pastor's role has a long-term relationship, an evangelist's role is short term and possibly leads the person somewhere else to find a long-term relationship.

How To Use This Book Moving Forward?

Read, Reflect, Revise, Implement, these are the four key things to bear in mind as you move forward. This book is designed to be interactive as much as possible. You will interact with seven chapters, each followed by a reflection. Read to learn new things and refresh what you already know. Reflect on what you read and pay close attention to areas that stood out to you for good or bad. After your reflection, consider ways you could or should revise your current plan for evangelism within the ministry. Finally, establish a plan for implementation.

In the end, you will circle back around to the EVA of evangelism. You will spend most of your time there as you consider ways to either Establish or strengthen your plan, study your Vicinity, and assume your Authority in the area God has given you.

This book is not to be a study done in isolation. It is important that while you may be the Pastor, or leader of the ministry, God never intended for you to work in Silos. The reflection may be individual and, in some cases, private. However, it is important that there be an established time where all members in the ministry gather to consider the wellbeing of the ministry.

PAUSE: Before moving on, go to your workbook and complete the corresponding reflection for this chapter.

EVAngelize

CHAPTER 1

Fresh Wind to Evangelism

If you are looking for a fresh start, a new or revised approach to connecting with your community through evangelism, then my prayer is that this book is the tool you need. When I think of fresh wind, I am thinking of something that has always been there but now viewed from a different point of view. You see, wind has always been in existence. You cannot see it, but you can see the results of its move. You know when the wind is blowing because the leaves are moving, the trees are swaying, debris is moved from one side to the other on the ground. Wind provokes movement. The absence of wind leaves to stillness. I don't know about you, but there is nothing worse than to stand outside on a hot day and there is no wind, fresh or not, to cool me down. There is a reaction in the atmosphere that transforms the stillness from what it was when there was no movement.

This chapter considers the need for movement, it does not mean that the movement is a novel idea but rather that it lends for a fresh perspective. It is a shift in paradigm, from what was once viewed one way is now looked at differently. Is it a duck or is it a rabbit?

Paradigms

For the purposes of this book, we will use the following as a working definition around what a paradigm is.

A paradigm is an attitude or mentality that has been ingrained in an individual stemming from culture, past experiences or exposures, teachings or understandings around a certain pattern of behavior.

In other words, embedded in the mentality or culture of certain religious groups, there is the mindset that if a woman wears pants, she is in sin or if a man pierces his ears he is acting as a woman. I care not to give an opinion on either example; however, I want us to capture the essence of the text. The word of God says that man will look at the outer appearance of a person, but God looks at the heart. So, with that text alone, we know that the pants will not be the sin for the woman or the erring the sin for the man. That's a paradigm. Question, what would happen if the one passing judgement were to sit and speak with the individuals being judged? Would they find them to be sinners in the heart or believers, more sold out for Christ with the compassion of Christ than they are?

When we think of wind and how it moves, we can also associate it with paradigms. Let me explain. Wind by itself is just wind. The wind today is the wind tomorrow. The leaves blow today as a result of the wind and tomorrow with more wind, the leaves continue to blow. Whether it is a north wind or a south wind, it will blow. So, what is the big deal? There is a truth behind the wind. When it blows, it does not move all of the leaves at the same velocity or level. The other day as I sat in my office looking out the window at the leaves being blown by the wind, I noticed that some leaves moved while others did not. Some leaves moved more swiftly while others did not. Now I know what you might be thinking, "What does that have to do with fresh wind or paradigm?" What makes some leaves blow and also lets others stay still. It is the same wind. Nothing is above the wind, nothing is holding the wind and funneling it to a certain direction, but nonetheless, some are getting moved more than others.

You see friends, God is a curious God, and the way He does things is far beyond our understanding. What I felt God revealing to me as I looked at the leaves, was this; the wind is blowing, and everything can be impacted by the same gust but only some of the leaves, branches, or trees are prepared to move on impact. Some will move faster than others but there will be a move. This is just like evangelism; everyone has the potential to be impacted by the release of the word but only some people are in position upon impact of the released word. The challenge is, how do you know who is ready and who is not? How do you know what word to release and or what testimony to give? What you do know is this. There must be a released word or testimony. When we look back at the tree analogy I gave earlier, if there was no wind then all the leaves would be stagnant and stay in one place with no progress. That's why you need to release the wind for progress to be seen by those in the right position to be impacted by the word. There are people who have been put in position to receive the word or testimony and that's why you cannot just release the word anywhere.

This chapter, Fresh Wind is not about making evangelism out to be something novel, a new idea. Since the days of scripture, evangelism has been key to the growth of the church. If we consider the way Jesus developed His ministry following His return from the wilderness, we will notice that He connected with men, women, and children of varying levels. He was able to minister, win their hearts not from an elevated post but rather through His ability to connect individually and personally with each. Fresh Wind is necessary simply because there are SO many churches that are rising up around us and still the larger population of our communities are unchurched or do not believe there is a need to attend a church.

When I started Flowing Rivers International Church, one thing was clear to myself and the team that was with me, we did not want to be just another church. We were tired of the same way of doing things. We were tired of 'doing' church. Now this might be offensive for some, however, if we can be transparent with ourselves, religion is pushing people away from the doors of churches. People these days do not want to go to a place where once again it is religion with a list of dos and don'ts in order to be saved, in order to congregate without being judged. People are looking for a real relationship and real intimacy with God. I believe as a pastor; I need to bring people into understanding the relationship that God is so desperately seeking from humanity. In the Garden of Eden, the creation of man was so that God could have that type of relationship with humanity. God does not want religion either, He is looking for intimacy, a close relationship between the creator and His creation.

Evangelism should be about bringing intimacy back into the equation of God meets man, man meets God. If an evangelist is as we defined above as one who brings good news, then the news must make sense to the recipient. We understand that the good news is the word of God leading to salvation through Jesus Christ. However, consider this, if I am a person who has been violated and know little or nothing about Jesus, how is giving me a tract, the traditional way of evangelism, going to help me? Just telling me Jesus loves me may not take away the scar of my violation, the scar is still there. However, if the person who is witnessing to me would be more relational as opposed to religious, sharing a story that touches the core of my hidden pain, I just might surrender in that moment. Now I understand that that is not the case for all. However, I have worked with hundreds if not thousands of young people over the years as they entered and exited the school system. I saw how impersonal and disconnected so many of them were. The connection I had with them was not me imposing myself on them but instead a result of the time I took to connect with them as young human beings.

We are in a day where the church is painted as so holy that there is a disconnect between the relational God we serve and the message we deliver. It is time for a fresh wind in how we deliver the Word of God.

As we consider Fresh Wind, there are three things to consider moving forward:

1. Establish a plan
2. Know your Vicinity
3. Walk in your Authority

In the next few chapters, we will look at the why of Evangelism from an organized and intentional perspective; where we are and who we are targeting; and, the reality of our authority over the community we are established in. I speak to you the reader as the Apostle Paul spoke to the church. Beloved, this message is for those who are aligned with a Kingdom vision. Simply put, if you do not believe that there is authority and power given to the church today to walk as in the days of the Apostles, this book might become difficult for you to engage in.

In the book of Ezekiel, the Lord asked the prophet, if he thought the dry bones could live again. We are talking about bones that once belonged to people with life and purpose. Bones that at one point believed and dreamed in many of the same things you believe and dream about right now. Not only were they dead, time had passed and now the only remains are dry bones. Something that for the natural eye is impossible became the subject of the faith of the prophet Ezekiel. If you have not read the story, please do so in Ezekiel, chapter 37. There is a point where under the Lord's leading, he called on the wind from the four corners of the earth, which is representative of the Holy Spirit. Not only did the dry bones come back together again, they lived again. The message here for the church is that all around us are dry bones, people who have lost hope, purpose and direction. If we the church see potential and not failure, our message will change from doctrine that is binding to one that is delivering. Question, how much access does the Holy Spirit of God have in your ministry? The answer to that question bears heavily on the movement of the Fresh Wind throughout your ministry.

PAUSE: Before moving on, go to your workbook and complete the respective reflection for this chapter.

CHAPTER 2

The EVA of Evangelism

"Eva is a female given name, the Latinate counterpart of English Eve, derived from a Hebrew name meaning "life" or "living one." It can also mean full of life or mother of life. It is the standard biblical form of Eve in many European languages." (https://en.wikipedia.org)

In agreement with the definition above, the name EVA derives from the name EVE meaning 'life', 'Living one' or 'mother of life.' This definition is in many ways, key to understanding the focus of this book about EVAngelism; giving emphasis to the first three letters, Establish, Vicinity and Authority. This chapter will put into context why these three letters lead to the foundation of what will build and strengthen your ministry team in the area of evangelism.

In the book of John where we see Jesus find and reinstate Peter to the group of now 11, Jesus engaged Peter in a series of questions that still ring true today. The fact is, most people read the text, but few truly understand what Jesus was asking. You see, Jesus was not interested in just any answer from Peter. He was looking for an answer that would assure Him of our readiness to serve His people. Let us look at the text.

15 When they had finished eating, Jesus said to Simon Peter, "Simon son of John, do you love me more than these?" "Yes, Lord," he said, "you know that I love you." Jesus said, "Feed my lambs." 16 Again Jesus said, "Simon son of John, do you love me?" He answered, "Yes, Lord, you know that I love you." Jesus said, "Take care of my sheep." 17 The third time he said to him, "Simon son of John, do you love me?" Peter was hurt because Jesus asked him the third time, "Do you love me?" He said, "Lord, you know all things; you know that I love you."

> *Jesus said, "Feed my sheep.*
> *(John 21:15-17 NIV)*

Jesus asked Peter three times, "Do you love me?" Peter answered three times, "Yes." However, what Jesus was saying to Peter in the translation of the first two times was, "Do you 'Agape' me, do you love me unconditionally.? Peter was responding that he loved the Lord, and he did but his love was the 'Philio' type of love. For those who are unfamiliar with this term, it is a love that is relational and with conditions. It is a love that leaves room for making a judgement on the extent to which you will love the person. Jesus was not asking Peter that. He wanted to know if he would love without condition, without judgement of exceptions. It was on the third try when Jesus said to Peter, "Do you love, Philio, me" that Peter understood. The third time, Peter was frustrated but awoken in understanding that Jesus was more interested in the type of love he would have for the people of God, 'sheep.' Peter's final response was yes, he "agape, loved" Him.

Today the genesis of evangelism is relegated to conditions and restrictions that almost make it impossible for people to really come to the Lord and want to stay. Please do not misunderstand this text, Agape love does not everything goes. God is a God of order and there are conditions to salvation that are not subjected to the opinions of man but to the direct instruction of the Word of God. Agape love opens the door for God's mercy and restoration, regardless of how far one has fallen, without judgement or rejection. The scriptures says in Romans 6:23, "All have sinned and fallen short of the glory of God…" So, we thank God for His grace, that without condition we can look at the next person with arms wide open and say, "Welcome." Now my friends, EVAngelism is saying we need to go back to the genesis, the beginning of evangelism, become more Christlike and establish a plan that will engage the communities around you, regardless of where you are.

The EVA of Evangelism is also saying, we must be sensitive to the original intent or understanding around evangelism, network it to the generation and communities we are serving to the extent without compromise we can reach them as Jesus intended. I think so many times we try to connect the old systems that were once effective to new communities, and new environments with the mentality that because it worked back in the day, it will work today as well. No, my friend, it will not. The system of the sixties or the seventies and on were effective because it was the demand of the time. Today there is a different demand, so how are we going to connect with today's communities? How are we going to bring life to a world of technology walking from door to door, park to park? Don't get me wrong in some moments, it can still be an effective tool, however, to win the hearts of today's generation, we need a net that connect in the stream of life they are flowing in. I am not saying to compromise the Word of God. I am not saying to water down the word or adjust the word to a pacified state that makes everyone happy. The word of God must be taught, and the Holy Spirit of God brings conviction as only He can. What I am saying is, we can't give steak to a baby, they do not have teeth to eat it. We can't give an unbeliever the Bible and expect them to just get saved because we gave them the book to read. At the end of the day, it is a book until the words become life and fill the heart of the ones reading it. That is the danger of unrelatable tracts. The best 'tract' we can use today is the relationship of relatability to where the person is in their current state and how an encounter with God can change their lives.

Jesus became relatable with those he met. He modeled evangelism through compassion, correction and love. He demonstrated to the apostles how to feed the hungry, how to heal the sick, how to love the rejected, how to teach the unteachable and the list goes on. In other words, the genesis of Evangelism is not how much you have in your hand but Who you have in your heart. In order to accomplish EVA of Evangelism, we MUST clothe our heart with Christ. He will fill us with the tools and the strategies that will allow for three blind men to be healed three different ways. We will connect with people, not the way we connected with the last person but rather looking each day at people as a new opportunity to win a soul for the kingdom. Having our hearts clothed with Jesus will also shift our mindset from the religious fulfillment of meeting a quota to relationship with people who, like us, were also made in His image and likeness. Having a heart like Christ will furthermore allow us to connect with brothers and sisters we use to look at and pass by on the job, the store, streets, or even family gatherings because they were different and now embrace them.

I can't help but think about the book of Zechariah.

3 Then he showed me Joshua the high priest standing before the angel of the LORD, and Satan standing at his right side to accuse him. 2 The LORD said to Satan, "The LORD rebuke you, Satan! The LORD, who has chosen Jerusalem, rebuke you! Is not this man a burning stick snatched from the fire?"3 Now Joshua was dressed in filthy clothes as he stood before the angel. 4 The angel said to those who were standing before him, "Take off his filthy clothes."

Then he said to Joshua, "See, I have taken away your sin, and I will put fine garments on you.
5 Then I said, "Put a clean turban on his head." So, they put a clean turban on his head and clothed him, while the angel of the LORD stood by.
Zechariah 3 (NIV)

This is a continuation of the love story of God for His creation. Testimony of God's mercy and redemptive grace towards humanity. The prophet states, "Is not this man a burning stick snatched from the fire?" For me and the for the purpose of this book, I look at this text and stand in awe of the fact that we are in a constant circle of fire. From the day we are born till the day we confess Christ and even thereafter. The adversary is constantly looking for ways to ensnare us, trap us into a web that leads us to a place of total and utter destruction. The grace of God is always, I have found, timely and intentional. If we look at the text. Joshua who stands in representation of humanity is a man filthily dressed, covered in the soot of the fumes of the fire, not a pretty site to look at. He represents all our sins, transgressions and iniquities all in one. But God! God in His mercy will still find the good and the why of rescue and go to the lengths to save us. We may look at the fire and the fumes with all the debris of rejection, but God looks at us and sees necessary process, and purpose for positioning.

The next couple of verses marks the power of this chapter. The EVA of EVAngelism. The dawning of a fresh approach to an age-old necessary practice, reaching the lost.

The instruction given to those around Joshua was twofold:

- Take off the filthy clothing from off him
- Put on a clean turban and fresh clothes

Let us pay attention to what is happening here, proximity and position. Let me explain. The only way to either take off the clothes and or put on a turban and fresh clothing is by getting close enough. It is not an us versus them stance. It is not stand in the pulpit, from an office or extend a wish that is going to get us close to the people, the Joshua's who need us. We must decide that every one of God's human creations are so important that we are willing to go when God says go. Now I am not being naive by telling you to go where God has not sent you. You need to pray; you need to have a vision and direction from God with the strategy on how and where you are to go. Even Jesus was intentional while He walked the earth and where He sent the disciples. I am saying, you will have moments of commissioning where you are called to go out and minister and when they come you need to have the heart to go even if the places you are sent are uncomfortable.

The next thing about this text is position. You must be able to get in position with the person or community if you are going to address them. This requires eyeballing people, and offices where you might be uncomfortable. Here is the thing, proximity only gets you to the door. Positioning allows you access to touch and interact on a personal level. The only way they could take off his clothes, clean him up and dress him was through a level of surrender that only comes through positioning. Think of it, would you allow just anyone to take off your clothes? Absolutely NOT. So, what would their position in your life need to look like for that to happen?

I believe, if we really take the time to act towards the Joshua's of the world, that God is going to be there beside us to give us favor. When people see that we are willing to recognize, not condemn the fire that surrounds them, prostitution, drugs, abuse, homicide, lying, stealing, etc. and still be willing to get close to them. They will not reject our hand and desire to helping them out of their filthy rags into something new.

Before you move on, let us reflect on this chapter on the EVA of evangelism. Be intentional to discuss where you were before reading this section and now that you have read it, how has it impacted your life? Try in this section to transparently look at your traditional or religious mindset towards evangelism and be willing to consider entering the dawning of a fresh approach to winning souls for the kingdom.

PAUSE: Before moving on, go to your workbooks and complete the respective reflection for this chapter.

CHAPTER 3

Steps to Establishing

"Where there is no vision, the people perish"
Proverbs 29:18
My people perish for lack of understanding"
Hosea 4:6

One of the most dangerous things I am observing these days is how easy people think it is to start a ministry. Let me explain. There are churches that rise every day. Some churches rise because someone gets up and believes God has called them. And He may have called them, but did He tell them to go when they went or go where they went? Some churches are the result of people forming a church within a church. There are those who warm benches and criticize how things are being done with the diabolic intent of pulling people towards themselves. David's own son did something of the sort. From within the palace, one of David's son, Absalom, began working up ways to deny the crown of his father. PAUSE: this is called the Absalom spirit. It is a spirit that overtakes a member, usually a leader, someone in position of influence. It works its way into the heart of that person and before long the church has been split in two, three or more. So today, we are seeing churches with a leader possessing the Absalom spirit. Why is this so important? In order to avoid clerical malpractice in the pulpit and give way to the healthy growth of a church, it is important to search the heart of the leadership.

Searching the heart of the leadership is both individual and collective. It is important for all involved to become naked before God when considering the origins of the church. What is the vision of the church? Who is the leadership? Are they equipped to lead? Does the church have a growth plan or is it enough to just show up for service and meetings? Is there a plan for ministerial development? Is there a plan for the church to shift from five to fifty or more? If I cannot sit with the pastor which is a deep-rooted mindset of so many, especially if they like me are from the "Islands." This is a tradition that essentially leads to the notion of, "If I cannot sit with the pastor or priest, who can I sit with based on my needs?" Did the church have a good or bad beginning? If the church had a bad beginning, and some churches do, the question must be asked, has it been healed? Has the pain of the past been eradicated? Are the leadership in servitude to Absalom?

I will take this moment to highlight three of the spirits that tend to destroy churches, one of which is the Absalom spirit, a spirit that works within the leadership. The second is the Jezebel spirit, the great puppeteer that works from the outside, manipulating the membership, turning their hearts away from truth, creating a false doctrine that shifts from the love of God to the love of Baal. The next is the Pharisee spirit, one that is religious in nature, doing everything possible to keep the status quo of what was. They will be more religious, condemning the new arrivals and burdening the ones who have history in the ministry with rules that makes loving and serving a great challenge. There are other spirits that attack the church, however, familiarity with these most prevalent spirits will help you as a leader understand what is going on in your ministry and how to move forward.

This chapter on ESTABLISH is about establishing a plan for your ministry to grow through EVAngelism. For that to be effective, an awareness of the ministry climate is key. If you as the pastor or ministry leader are not aware of the spiritual oppositions you have within the spiritual and natural walls of your ministry, how will you be able to go out and really win souls? When souls enter your church, where will they go? Will these individuals be better off in your environment or on the streets, within the community where you found them? Friends, the whole idea of bringing someone into the ministry is as we saw in the case of Joshua in the book of Zechariah, all about proximity and position. Catching them and bringing them in requires A LOT of work. What will they see different in your ministry that will cause them to stay? How will you communicate that to them besides handing them a pamphlet and having them read it? This is important to consider as we delve into the meat and potatoes of this chapter.

This chapter along with the following two, will have moments of TESTIMONIALS. Within the testimonials, I will share some of the things my team and I implemented in the foundation building of our church and also about our approach to evangelism. Not all sections will have testimonials, however, the sections that do have them will serve as a guide to understand that this is not just a book that is abstract in application but a walking guide for my church, Flowing Rivers International Church, as well.

Establish your vision – your WHAT

"Where there is no vision, the people perish"
Proverbs 29:18

The church MUST have a vision that clearly defines the why of their existence. Who are they and why are they in the city, community, or region they are in? I am a firm believer that when God establishes a church within a community it serves to add value leading to transformation. I do not believe a church is to just occupy a post in a corner of the city, holding services every week and having no impact on the community they are in. The impact of each church does not have to look the same, but there must be an impact, a sign that the Kingdom of God has arrived to that area. The goal in getting at or understanding the purpose of being assigned to a community is to have a clear vision.

In the book of Luke chapter 11, we see where Jesus makes a clear yet profound statement on what happens when the Kingdom of God enters a city. In our day we would say, when the church is established in a city.

14 Jesus was driving out a demon that was mute. When the demon left, the man who had been mute spoke, and the crowd was amazed. 15 But some of them said, "By Beelzebul, the prince of demons, he is driving out demons." 16 Others tested him by asking for a sign from heaven.

> *17 Jesus knew their thoughts and said to them: "Any kingdom divided against itself will be ruined, and a house divided against itself will fall. 18 If Satan is divided against himself, how can his kingdom stand? I say this because you claim that I drive out demons by Beelzebul. 19 Now if I drive out demons by Beelzebul, by whom do your followers drive them out? So then, they will be your judges. 20 But if I drive out demons by the finger of God, then the kingdom of God has come upon you.*
> *(Luke 11:14-20, NIV)*

Jesus is making it clear that prior to His arrival, the works they were seeing were demonic in nature, led by Beelzebul. The demons were attacking under a command of their leader so when Jesus appeared on the scene, He was demonstrating a work greater than Beelzebul. He drove out the mute spirit out of the man, something surprising to everyone around. Did you know that when people are not accustomed to seeing something new it can lead them to fear and not just that, lead to torment? Jesus boldly said to them that if Satan was against Himself then His kingdom would be divided and therefore would not stand. It would be ludicrous for Satan to divide his own kingdom, that's poor governance. I love what Jesus says in v20 "But if I drive out demons by the finger of God, then the Kingdom of God has come upon you." (Luke 11:20, NIV)

When a church enters a community, it is representative of the Kingdom of God arriving to that place. There MUST be evidence, fruit that demonstrates they are different from the culture that previously existed. When I think of small communities where there are over 100 churches with minimal to no change within the community, I stop to wonder, has the Kingdom of God arrived? If the demons are being cast out and staying in the place they are cast out from, has the Kingdom of God arrived? Every church, mine included, cannot be another building or space within a community holding cultic gatherings with the hopes of being better than the next one. That provokes a competitive spirit that serves to further divide and distance the church from the purpose of God.

What is a vision?

Let us begin by defining a vision.

In the dictionary, the word vision is defined as "the act or power of seeing…something seen in a dream or trance…a supernatural appearance that conveys revelation…a thought, concept or object formed by the imagination." With the natural eye,
The prophet Ezekiel was taken in visions as the Lord revealed to him the restoration of the temple area.

" 2 In the visions of God He took me into the land of Israel and set me on a very high mountain; on it toward the south was something like the structure of a city. 3 He took me there, and behold, there was a man whose appearance was like the appearance of bronze. He had a line of flax and a measuring rod in his hand, and he stood in the gateway.

4 And the man said to me, "Son of man, look with your eyes and hear with your ears, and [a]fix your mind on everything I show you; for you were brought here so that I might show them to you. Declare to the house of Israel everything you see."
(Ezekiel 40:2-4, NKJV)

Notice that what Ezekiel saw had not yet come to pass. He was taken in a vision to a place that was yet to come but God revealed to the prophet a foreshadowing of hope. It would be a message of all is not lost, there was coming a day when what has been destroyed would one day be restored.

A vision then, is often the act of foreshadowing what is to come. It is a revelation or unveiling of those things that are hidden to the naked eye.

The prophet Joel, says regarding visions, that, "…it shall come to pass afterward that I will pour out My Spirit on all flesh; Your sons and your daughters shall prophesy, your old men shall dream dreams, your young men shall see visions. 29 And also on My menservants and on My maidservants, I will pour out My Spirit in those days." (Joel 2:28-29, NKJV) What is important to note here is so many believe that these last days have already come to pass but, we are still living in those days Joel prophesied. When the Apostle Peter referred to these days in Acts 2, not only was he referring to the manifestation of the Holy Spirit upon the 120 but the fact that we are now in a time where what was shown in a vision has now become real. What this is saying to the church today is what was revealed in the old testament was just a shadow of what is happening today.

What we see in a vision is not a natural occurrence, it is much bigger than that. For the purpose of this study material, we consider visions as revelations that are supernatural in nature, revealing whether in dream, during prayer or meditation, where the curtains are lifted from off a hidden truth bearing an impending reality. As we move forward, we want you, the reader to bear in mind the goal of this book, which is to bring us into an understanding of what a vision is as well as the vision of the Terika Smith Ministries to include Flowing Rivers International Church and all those who are a part of the body.

As we saw in both texts, the visions were reliant on someone seeing or experiencing them. Therefore, visions are divine or supernatural revelations made to men, referring to humanity. Many people receive visions but do not understand what is going on. We believe it requires faith to really agree and receive the vision being revealed. If not careful, one might confuse a vision to a nightmare, or a dream be it bad or good.

Hosea 4:6 tells us that the consequence of lack of vision is failure or destruction. What is he referring to and how does that apply to us today? Visions as we have learned are deposited in a person. The goal then is to put that vision into motion. Whenever God reveals something, we can be certain that there is an expected outcome. The challenge is in those areas where there is lack of faith. So, if we agree with Hosea, he is saying that lack of revelation, causes people to make mistakes which lead to detrimental consequences. Visions not only reveal truth but promotes understanding as to how to proceed regardless the plan or decisions that need to be made.

Our base text, Habakkuk 2:2-3 states, "Write the vision and make it plain on tablets, that he may run who reads it. 3 For the vision is yet for an appointed time; But at the end it will speak, and it will not lie. Though it tarries, wait for it; Because it will surely come, It will not tarry." It reminds us that first we must catch the vision and then act on it.

- Write the vision
- Make it plain or understandable for the reader
- Make it accessible in a forum where others can get to it

A person who believes the vision that has been revealed to them, regardless of how audacious it might be needs to take the time and put it on paper. Faith sets in motion the act of simply writing it down and sharing it with someone. I used to throw the discus when I was in track and field. The thing about the discus is the buildup of momentum as you move through the circle. The quicker you move through the circle with your eyes focused on the goal the greater the impact on the release. In other words, the vision becomes more alive in a person or group when placed in strategic places and the more it is discussed the more alive it becomes. I used to tell my athletes, "If you can see it in your mind's eye, you can do it. If you can see yourself throwing far, then you can do it. It all starts with seeing it and then believing it is possible." Think of it, a car is not built without a plan, a plan is not built without a plan nor is a house built without a plan. That plan is derived from a vision.

In sum, a vision is an internal revelation with an external manifestation. For the body of faith, it is what God deposits in you that you then realize to the world around you.

Going back to the discus, throwing far required seeing yourself throwing the distance, having a marker that you can aim at, being motivated by people who believe in you and being willing to put in the extra work to accomplish your goal. There is a great correlation between the discus and vision setting. I did not see it before, but I do now.

Vision setting, therefore requires several things:

- Believing the revelation is possible
- See it in the invisible before it can manifest in the visible
- Establish a goal or plan to see it come to pass
- Spend time with people who believe the same as you or can see where you are going and lend support to seeing it come to pass God revealed to Ezekiel what He was going to do with the temple before Israel, it had not yet come to pass but we read about it today and know that we are closer to it coming to pass as we follow the signs of those who believe what they saw.

Testimonial: When our church began, we never sat to discuss how we could competitively look and sound different from any other church. We were very focused on finding God's plan and purpose for our lives. We wanted to know what God wanted and how HE wanted us to get it done. I must tell you, that was not easy. We wanted a name that was not traditional and relevant to purpose. So, what do I mean by relevant to purpose? Nike sells shoes and lots of other items, every piece of Nike product has the Nike brand on it. You cannot confuse Nike with Converse. It's THEIR brand. They are always looking for ways to live up to their brand, creating timeless clothing that regardless the generation, they can appreciate it. This concept does not always cross over to the church world. We wanted to make sure that our name, and our brand reflected the heart of God for our lives. We wanted to ensure that wherever we go, the name becomes alive into the hearts of everyone present.

Flowing Rivers International Church was a name birthed out of prayer and searching God for direction. We are a people who believe firmly in the Holy Spirit and His move. We know and understand that the text Ezekiel 47:8 is referring to more than just waters flowing from beneath the temple but symbolic as well of the Holy Spirit. We were smitten by the part in scripture where it says that where the water touches it will bring life. THAT IS POWERFUL! We wanted and still do, to be THAT church that brings life wherever we go. No, we are not perfect human beings, but we have a Holy Spirit who is. It took us close to three years to really hammer down our vision for the church. Yes, a few years, we began with something simple and sincere but that lacked clarity on the true essence of who we were to become as a body. See our vision statement in the appendix. We learned that it was fine to continuously review and revise the vision, if for no other reason, so that our decisions were aligned with what God told us. We also wanted to make sure that our church community continuously gained an understanding of who we were as a body and why we do what we do.

Establish your purpose – your WHY

Vision is key to purpose. Every church must have purpose and that purpose can't be to fill the pews. Jesus said His purpose was to do the will of the One who sent Him. Never did we see Jesus preach about Himself. Never in scripture did we see Jesus take credit for the works He did while on earth. He always gave God the credit, the one who sent Him.

Why does your church exist? This is a big question and quite honestly, difficult to answer by many. Some churches are started out of a split, disgruntled members deciding to leave and ready do it better elsewhere. Some start because someone has a call and instead of waiting on God for timing and positioning jump to get started; sometimes they remain low in numbers, primarily their family and maybe one or two others. Then there are churches that are planted within a community by a larger body with the goal of spreading their reach in the church world. Some churches have the Amos 3:3 beginning, "How can two walk together unless they be in agreement" or like Paul and John Mark, they did not continue together due to philosophical and spiritual immaturity and because of that it was best they go in separate directions. Both continued in ministry and were later reunited.

What is the purpose of your church in the community God has placed it in? If you placed yourself there you will struggle to answer this question. If God has placed you there then there will be alignment with what you are doing and who flows into your church's doors. What makes you different from the church across the street, down the block or anywhere in your proximity? Was it better for you to start a new church in that community? How do you know? Why didn't you just join the one next to you, down the street or in your building? If you are new, what provoked your newness? Did you just graduate from seminary and felt this was your season? Were you sent by a larger body and they released you into that community? If so, what is their purpose for you there?

The questions on purpose are many and there are more. It is important that every church's pastor/leader grasp the why of their existence in order to really impact the community around them. Do not just settle that you were able to spend a day at the park witnessing, that's good, or help a homeless person in your community, that's good too. Guess what, so are others. Purpose, results in impact, and legacy.

Impact: We are defining it as the effect or influence of one person, thing, or action, on another

Legacy: We are defining legacy as something handed down by a predecessor, an inheritance, a will

Purpose: is the ability to have impact and establish a replicable legacy to leave a lasting impact. In the church world it is not about family inheritance, the anointing and calling of God on one's life is not passed on in a will, that is GOD's prerogative. It is, however, the divine influence of God upon a community in which God's purpose is being carried out. The skeptic would say here, "Aren't we all doing God's purpose?" There is a point to that, good, bad or indifferent. However, my focus, in this book is speaking as the Lord leads to the church community on a fresh approach to Evangelism and why things may or may not work. No vision, no purpose equals no direction.

Testimonial: FRI was started out of a clarion call that my time had come to an end at the church I was pastoring for over five years. From the outside, the ending looked ugly and for some embarrassing, however, we would all learn, myself included that it was a necessary exit in order to step into the purpose God brought me to New England for. If I can confess, having a church in the City of Lawrence where I live is not what I wanted. I, along with the small group I was pastoring at the time searched for locations away from Lawrence, BUT GOD! He had other plans for us and brought us to a place we do not deserve but daily we see His hand at work. We are not in this city to be another of over 100 churches. We are clear that we are to add value to the work of the Lord in this city. We are clear that the Kingdom of God has arrived in the city. It sounds bold and audacious knowing there is such a wealth of history in this city, however, what we are saying is simply this. The waters that flow from beneath the temple that brings life to whatever it touches has arrived. We are ONLY like us, here to accomplish what He has established us to accomplish. Our purpose is not to go into other camps, see what they have, and we do not have to compete with them within the city and beyond. A designer's original is not a replication, it is unique.

If God has established your ministry in the community where it sits, what makes your church unique? How are you communicating your uniqueness? Now that your wheels are turning, consider this, your vision drives your purpose and your purpose drives your plan. You will find that chaos resides in initiatives without direction.

Establish your plan – your HOW

What is your plan for your ministry? Do you want a traditional church or nontraditional church? Do you want to establish the church in a rural, urban or city community? Who will you involve in the process? In the business world, this is part of your strategic planning for your company. Yes, your church needs a strategic plan as well. Here are some helpful steps you can take:

Establish your ministry – your VEHICLE (tracs, in person, video, from the pulpit, etc.)

When establishing your ministry, I recommend that you are clear of the vision God has given you. Did He deposit in you a Full church model or a cell group model?

- Full church model is defined for the purposes of this work as a church that is representative of the traditional church layout as we know it. The church would have a senior pastor, other ministers or leaders, ministries reflective of the body, growth or maintenance plan, etc.

- Cell group model is defined here as a small Bible study group that may or may not grow into the full church model. In some cases, it may become the actual church but without the politics of the full church model as is described above.

It is of utmost importance when considering the type of ministry the Lord has deposited in you that you are true to it. Remember, the plan is NOT yours, it is His, so the blessing of the plan taking effect lies in your ability as a leader to rest on His leading.

Establish your team – your WHO

Not everyone sits at the initial table, it is important to have some people with kindred spirit sitting at the table with you. Not everyone who sits at the table is there with you. There will be people there with hidden agendas. I have learned that it is not for me to focus on the agendas of others but on the plan of God. You might be scratching your head now and wondering why, aren't those people important to identify and pluck out? Not necessarily. Hidden agendas keep you on your knees and focused on the plan of God. In a parable, Jesus told his disciples the following;

"24 Jesus told them another parable: "The kingdom of heaven is like a man who sowed good seed in his field. 25 But while everyone was sleeping, his enemy came and sowed weeds among the wheat, and went away. 26 When the wheat sprouted and formed heads, then the weeds also appeared. 27 "The owner's servants came to him and said, 'Sir, didn't you sow good seed in your field? Where then did the weeds come from?' 28 "'An enemy did this,' he replied. "The servants asked him, 'Do you want us to go and pull them up?' 29 "'No,' he answered, 'because while you are pulling the weeds, you may uproot the wheat with them. 30 Let both grow together until the harvest. At that time, I will tell the harvesters: First collect the weeds and tie them in bundles to be burned; then gather the wheat and bring it into my barn.'"

Matthew 13:24-30 (NIV)

In the parable, Jesus was letting them know that the wheat and the weeds have purpose together. You see, there is risk in pulling up the weeds, you can mistakenly pull up wheat. By trying so hard to get rid of the ones with hidden agendas you might develop an attitude of distrust so strong that you miss the one who is really an asset to your ministry but needs strong guidance. Judas was at the table with Jesus, but he looked like the others and was taught by Jesus the same way the other eleven were taught. Jesus knew he would betray Him, but not once did Jesus treat him differently. It is a weird place to be as a leader today, not having anywhere close to the depth of compassion that Jesus had but we have a divine responsibility to seek it daily. The compassion of Christ allows us to see as God sees and work with the people, He sends us.

As the leader, do not be quick to assign roles to people because they are at the table. If they are family be extra careful. Remember, this is kingdom business not family business so let the King lead your decision making. Human error in assigning roles can lead to what I call, ministerial fatalities. No one has rights to the governance of a church but the one assigned by the 'governor', the Lord himself. I cannot stress enough, you have got to know that God has called you, it is ONLY then that you will seek His leading. When scripture says, "touch not mine anointed, and do my prophets no harm" (1 Chronicles 16:22 KJV) it says to me that when you are called of God you become His anointed. This is NOT licensed to do whatever you want, misuse or abuse the ministry or the people of God. Nor does it mean you will be perfect and free from fall, but rather it is saying you are under the care and watch of someone greater than you. When you mess up, and you will, your account is to God. It is because you are called to be His anointed, anyone who interferes with His plan for your life will not have to report to you but to HIM. That my friend is a dangerous place to be.

Establish your timeframe – your WHEN

When will you launch your ministry is the big question? I don't think there is ever a perfect textbook time as to when to launch your ministry. I do, however, believe that there is a God time to launch. Now what is a God time? A God time is the time when the overwhelming peace of God rests upon you like the Holy Spirit in the form of a dove resting on Jesus, identifying Him as the Son of God. It is that moment when you know within your heart that God is saying, "Launch out." Step out into the deep waters, let yourself go so deep within that there is none of you left, just Him.

Testimonial

I remember when we were getting ready to launch our church. Yes, it was scary, especially under the circumstances of our birth but there was that overwhelming peace of God that told me it was the right thing and the right time. I had a group of people at the table. I was not looking for those with hidden agendas, I was focused on HIS agenda. It did not take us very long, four days to be exact, to put the church together. We did not know how many people we would have; we just knew it was the season of our birthing. I was still in the birthing fluid of my previous season and yet was stepping into a new season. It was scary. I was not in control! That's my point on no perfect timing. On a normal day, in a normal scenario, it would have made practical sense to wait a while, heal and then return to the pulpit. That was not the case, God timed it in such a way that before I could bleed, I was healed. Don't try this as home! Yes, before I could bleed, God had already prepared me to not only withstand the storm but to also launch out into the deep.

On our first Sunday, God sent us 52 people, unprecedented especially since we had not embarked on evangelism in any way. I had a team; we had a location and He sent the people. Some have moved to different locations for different reasons over the years, but our number never went down. We are now in our fifth year and let's just say our children church alone has many Sundays with 52 or more children. This is not the norm so again, do not try this at home. Try it in God, trust His timing and launch when He says go.

After you have launched, it is important to have established times or seasons within the ministry where you will engage your team into a follow-up or evaluation of the progress of the ministry. How are your pastors, leaders and volunteers doing? How is the community outreach? Are you spending more than you are bringing in? Are you and the team willing to keep going? I hope the answer is yes to the latter. If God told you to go, then trust that He will see you through the trials. If you made the wrong turn, acknowledge it, pick yourself up and get back on track. Be willing to admit before God your mistakes, He already knows but cannot do anything until you invite Him in.

PAUSE: Before moving on, go to your workbooks and complete the corresponding reflection for this chapter.

CHAPTER 4

Knowing your Vicinity

As a child growing up in Jamaica, one of the most memorable moments was the time spent with the neighborhood kids. We did it all! We played in the streets, climbed the little hills and used cardboard boxes as our version of sleds. In those boxes we would slide down the hills, thinking nothing of it, it was heaven. We knew every family on the block, every family in the surrounding community. If there was a child there our age, we knew them and their parents. While our culture was not open to many sleep overs, we spent long hours outside playing, telling stories and eating whatever fruit was in season.

One day, I was returning home from school with my neighborhood friends. Out of nowhere came a speeding army jeep, I lived on the military base called Up Park Camp, a part of the Jamaican Defense Force in Kingston. This soldier was going so fast that he hit me. I was left unconscious. My father learned about it; it was the talk of the town. My father was a very high ranking official in the Jamaican Defense Force. Everyone, and anyone had heard about him and knew where he lived. Word got to him quickly and the long story made short, my accident was responsibly handled, and I am here today to tell the story.

I do not recall how many families lived in that community, but I recall this. It did not matter where I went or where my siblings went, just the mention of our last name lead to the question of whose children we were. Everyone in the community knew us. Outside of the military base in the local proximity or among individuals who were familiar with the Jamaican Defense Force at the time recognized and knew who he was. We knew the community and the community knew us well. Should I say, the community knew our father well?

I share this story as I consider our heavenly father. The community of humanity has a global understanding of who He is. Even though some reject Him, some question His existence and others are trying to play the balance beam of who He is without interrupting the status quo of their existence. There is a truth that everywhere you go you can engage in a conversation around God, who He is, where He is and how do we know He is real. The list is lengthy, but we are clear about this one thing, it is a topic that will provoke a healthy discussion, good or bad. If we keep this in perspective in terms of neighborhoods and communities, it does not matter the language, culture, or social dynamics, wherever the conversation comes up around faith or religion, God is at the center.

I did not understand why the Lord lead me down this road on my childhood at first, but now I do. You see, neighborhoods, vicinities, communities are moved and understood by common denominators. In the community where I grew up, my dad for a little girl was my common denominator. In our society, God is a common denominator. It does not matter the life that one leads, everyone has an opinion about who God is. That is AWESOME! I understand that there have been laws to publicly remove prayer and God out of written and published documents but isn't it interesting, in order to remove GOD, you have to have an understanding of why He was there in the first place. I add, how can you remove someone who you cannot see?

In this book, God has led me to have us look at vicinity in a novel way, novel to me and perhaps to yourself. He wants us to look at common denominators, what is it that will make the hearts and minds of man turn to talk? Wherever you go, regardless the echelon of society, what will be the common denominator? Vicinities have silent rules, silent codes, there are people who are behind the scenes making all the decision while others are in the forefront trying to navigate the waters of their surroundings. When you live in a vicinity for a lifetime, it gets to know you and you get to know it. You know how to move about, where to go and what to say. You also know what not to say, where not to go and who to stay away from. You learn these rules through the classroom of life, walking the streets of your neighborhoods, spending time in the barbershops or salons, networking with the decision makers while at times observing or avoiding the non-decisionmakers. I understand these are general statements, however there are truths in them.

Testimonial

When I moved from Jamaica to Illinois, it was a very difficult transition. I was a child, I left all my friends and MY VICINITY, my neighborhood, my language and my culture to go to a place I did not know. Yes, the people around me primarily spoke English but it was not the English we were taught in school while in Jamaica. I felt like a fish out of water. From my years as an educator and working with children who also were from other countries, I can tell you, they shared the same sentiments. As a child for me, the common denominator was the fact that we were children and as such we played the games kids played, took the same classes and ate in the same cafeteria. Outside of that, we were on opposite sides of the tracks. Fast forward to where I am now, it feels like the same cycle all over again. As an adult, I am in a community that was foreign to me when I arrived. With the people who surrounded me at the time and to some extent even now, it is not the inbred interests that would move a person to want to spend time together. Our common language is in what I do. It sounds crazy but as the Lord is pointing this out to me, I can hear Him say, "You won't win souls by who you are but by what you do." WHAT, really God? That was the first thought that popped in my head when He told me that. There is GREAT truth to this. I confess, who I am does not matter, what I do does. Who you are does not matter, but what you do, does.

Who vs What

As we look at the word vicinity, it is an area immediately surrounding something. In other words, when we consider vicinity for a ministry, we are looking at what is close to the ministry within a certain mile radius. As God has planted your church, my church, in a community it is important to grasp this simple truth in order to proceed with His work. Who you are in the community has its weight and can possibly draw a big crowd. The challenge is that that crowd might be there for you. They may never hear the name Jehovah God or even acknowledge Him in earnest as being their God. Their focus is on what is going on in your life as the leader, pastor, Bishop, etc., as opposed to who is behind you. You see, sometimes, who you are can lead to a lot of ego, pride and a ton of self. What you do can provoke a why question that will lead to the open dialogue where, "Had it not been for God in your life, you would not be who you are and where you are.

I want to be clear, you as an individual are important. You as a mouthpiece of God; is what you do to lift HIM up. I can take no credit for where God has me now. My life has taken so many turns and quite honestly, I have had some questions for God. I understood this, without God in my life and without Him leading my every step even when I fall down, I would not be where He has me now. My what has become greater than my who.

I'll let you in on a little secret. Regardless the community you are in, most people may not be interested in who you are but what you do may always pull a listening ear. The what is powerful; it has the potential to become the key denominator in God positioning you to conquer a city or a nation. Additionally, if you are doing a what, there is someone greater Who is behind you, charting the course of your steps. When God told Joshua that everywhere his foot stepped, He had given him that land, Joshua the leader was not the key denominator, his obedience to the One who sent him was. By Joshua obeying God, God was the "who" and Joshua was the "what."

Know your neighborhood, know your hood

In this book, I want you to consider that there are two types of neighborhoods, the one you grew up in and the one God has put you in. I understand that there are so many directions we could go in to discuss neighborhood, however, where the Lord is leading me is to stay clear of the theory and delve into the practical. Deep theory has the dangerous potential of putting the mind and heart of man in the middle while leaving out the most important person, the Almighty Himself. Evangelism in your Vicinity is not about theory, it is practical. As the Lord is leading me, let us consider the nuances around where you grew up as one vicinity and where God placed you. I want us to keep in mind, we are looking at our overall ministry and building a plan that is personal that will lead to growth and impact according to the model of God, Mathew 28:18-20

Where did you grow up?

A prophet is not welcomed in his own community. I reflect on Jesus, all you could hear was, "Isn't that Joseph's son?" They didn't acknowledge that He was the son of God, but rather the one they knew as He was growing up. They did not look at the fact that they may have known Jesus as He was growing up, but He was now a different person. People in the community you come from will remember you for the family you came from, the things you did growing up, the good things you did and especially the mistakes you made. Do you recall my testimony I shared earlier? I am not sure if now as a minister of the gospel I could go back to that same community and preach the Gospel of Jesus Christ. I should say, I could not go back there under the common denominator which was my father. I would have to go as a vessel of God to deliver His word. Will they receive me because I am Jamaican? Probably not. Will they receive me because I once ran those streets? Maybe not. Will they receive me because I am preaching the Word of God? Maybe. If God tells me to go, I must understand that I am no longer going back to that place as the person who left. I am now going there a representative of the Kingdom of God. My focus is on HIM, not me.

When you leave a place, you can always count on the fact that you have personal memories of the place. Sometimes the nostalgia of being in that place brings back memories that makes you smile, laugh or cry. You may even find yourself overwhelmed with emotions. What you do with all those emotions when you are in that place will influence greatly the outcome of the visit.

When you return to where you came from, gauge your movements:

- Why am I back?
  o Personal visit?
  o Divine assignment?
- Who was I when I was here?

- What should I do to avoid reverting to that person knowing I am on a mission beyond me?
- If you are not alone, you are a ministry, why did you choose that vicinity?
- Who do you know that would potentially serve as a good network?

  o Did God send you to them?
  o Are they a good network because of childhood memories or divine assignment?

- Where in the community did you go back to?
    o Is it the same place or has it changed?
    o Is the culture the same today as when you grew up there?
    o Is this still YOUR hood?

It is so important to ask these questions and process them through with your team, if you are a ministry, or you can also have a heart to heart with God. You cannot begin a God given assignment with an emotional agenda. In like fashion, you cannot begin an emotional agenda and then assign it to God, it just does not work.

Where did God put you?

When God puts you in a vicinity, He is strategic, intentional and timely. God may put you back in your old community, but it will always be in HIS timing. Israel did not cross the Jordan with Moses because it was not the time for them to cross. It was a familiar place they had been. Because of rebellion, they could not cross. They would have to wonder in the desert for 40 years and from there all the warring age men would die. Those who returned would be a new generation, ready to head the voice of the Lord. When God puts you in a community, a Vicinity, He puts you in a place that has been waiting for you. They may not know you by name. They may not know you by appearance. They may not know you by credentials nor do they care. BUT when a person is looking for something, when a community is looking for something, the moment they can identify it, it might scare them at first but with time and persistence there will be an embrace.

To every church leader, minister, member who knows God has put them in a place they do not understand, just trust the One who sent you and LET HIM LEAD. Sometimes the places God puts you do not reflect the places you would want to go. sometimes the places you want to go are not the places God wants you to go. I have seen so many people decide on where they are going with the false understanding that it is what God wanted. I have seen people try with frustration trying to do the work of the Lord and believing they are walking in His will. From experience I will tell you, the work of the Lord is arduous and can at times be challenging in the flesh to uphold. However, when God is in the middle of that work, your one truth is if He has given you the land, you will fight some battles, but they are battles that have already been won.

Principalities

Before we proceed to the next chapter on Authority, I want to address a very real point regarding Vicinities. Every vicinity, just like it has a physical authority governing the community be it a mayor, a counselor, an alderman, etc., they have been given the right to govern that city. Who gave them that power? Who appointed/anointed them to the position of office they are in? The answer is the people did, the people who reside within that community did. If they voted or remained in silence during the voting period, their silence gave the green light. Why is this important for us to consider? There is relationship with what happens in the physical with the spiritual. Spiritual authorities do not take up residence in a community unless the spiritual community puts them there. Let me explain. I can see your eyes open wide here.

I see so many churches and religious organizations do amazing things in communities to help the community. Often the work only serves to pacify or create a workable environment that can be harmonious for all. So, what is the problem with doing that? There is not a problem in working together, it must be done. I ask the question however, if light and darkness are working together, how can there be a common denominator? Who will in the end take the lead? When electing an official, there is not compromised to say two can win and then work out the responsibilities of each winner. One person wins. Why is it in the spiritual world of governance, the church world, that we compromise to the point where decisions are made for the church? The church is not participant in the process, not understanding ownership of the vicinity they are assigned to until it is too late.

Let us consider once more Mathew 28:1-20 "Then Jesus came to them and said, 'All authority in heaven and on earth has been given to me. Therefore, go and make disciples of all nations, baptizing them in the name of the Father and of the Son and of the Holy Spirit, and teaching them to obey everything I have commanded you. And surely I am with you always, to the very end of the age.'" Jesus just told His disciples that ALL authority was given to Him. That means regardless the vicinity, regardless the region, Jesus' authority supersedes ALL authority. Now understand, we the church cannot go around like a person or entity that has lost its mind declaring I have all authority so bow down to me. No, instead, it is walking in the confident humility that as God IS a God of order and He respects the law of the land, He also has established His church to restore the original intent of order to humanity. I chuckle as I consider the fact that man has more fear of the earthly government than the heavenly government. I chuckle in knowing that God has literally, through his Son released a level of governance to us that if we just understood it we would not need to fight one with the other but establish the order in the spiritual so that the earthly can be guided…….

In my book, there are several things the church is called to do and not called to do.

The church is called to:

- Bring light to whichever community it is assigned to
- Be a door and place of refuge for the world

- To govern the spiritual territory of the land it inhabits
- To work in all offices of society, lending a hand to the overall wellbeing of the community
- Establish the principles for life regardless the racial, cultural or social status of the individuals therein

The church is not called to:

- Work absent from the community that surrounds it
- Become a world of its own that is unable to interact with the world outside
- Compromise its foundational principles to meet the demands of the society, that being creating access to where the community determines the rules of the church. The word of God determines the rules of the church.

This list could be much lengthier. The point is that when God places the church into a community, it has a divine responsibility to have impact over the spiritual governance of that community first and foremost.

PAUSE: Before moving on, go to your workbooks and complete the reflection accompaniment for this chapter.

CHAPTER 5

Knowing your Authority

7 Calling the Twelve to him, he began to send them out two by two and gave them authority over impure spirits. 8 These were his instructions: "Take nothing for the journey except a staff—no bread, no bag, no money in your belts. 9 Wear sandals but not an extra shirt. 10 Whenever you enter a house, stay there until you leave that town. 11 And if any place will not welcome you or listen to you, leave that place and shake the dust off your feet as a testimony against them." 12 They went out and preached that people should repent. 13 They drove out many demons and anointed many sick people with oil and healed them.
Mark 6:7-13 (NIV)

18 Then Jesus came to them and said, "All authority in heaven and on earth has been given to me. 19 Therefore go and make disciples of all nations, baptizing them in the name of the Father and of the Son and of the Holy Spirit, 20 and teaching them to obey everything I have commanded you. And surely, I am with you always, to the very end of the age."
Matthew 28:18-20 (NIV)

This chapter on authority is by far my favorite. This is the chapter where I enjoy just knowing that Jesus won. Yes, I said it, Jesus won. He won the battle against Satan. He won the battle against the grave. He won the battle against death. He won the battle against sickness. He won the battle against disease. He won the battle against opposition and oppression. He won the battle against mental illness. He won the battle against generational curses. He won the battle. There is no problem too great or too small for him. Jesus is the beginning and the ending. He is the first and the last. He is the Son of God, He is God the Son, He is our breasted one, He is infinitely awesome. I can go on and on as you can see. You can probably hear the passion in my words.

I am passionate about the power of God through Jesus Christ, not because I love power but because I understand that the walk of the believer is a constant and daily spiritual battle. It is a battle that we do not fight in the flesh but in the spirit. You might say, "If you do not understand scripture, how do you fight in the spirit? Well the short answer is, you do not fight, but Jesus does.

The scripture says, "the weapons of our warfare are not carnal but mighty through God for the pulling down of strongholds." (2 Corinthians 10:4, KJV) Now that is a whole sermon all by itself, a lengthy teaching for the one who do not understand. However, in short form I will say this.

The walk of the believer is in constant opposition to the life they lived while in the world. The enemy is always looking for ways to pull you back to the place you were before you came to Christ. Now capture this, before you confessed Jesus Christ as Lord of your life, you my friend had another lord. Satan was your lord. Yup, it is that simple. You can't see him, but he led you in to doing things, living a way that was contrary to the plan God has for your life.

The moment you came to Christ, you renounced him. I would venture to say, he was dethroned. When a king is dethroned, someone else takes over the kingdom. You essentially kicked Satan out of your heart and gave sole rulership to Jesus. You cannot see Satan and you cannot see Jesus, but you know the two exist, right? You know that there is good and there is evil right? Now if we put it all in context. If you do not wrestle with flesh and blood but against the spiritual world then simply put, you are not physically wrestling. The King inside of you is wrestling with the king that is coming against you. Praise God! I look at it this way, you are as strong as the latitude you give the King inside of you to fight for you.

What does the above have to do with authority? The answer is this, if God has assigned you to a location, a community, a region or a nation. The assignment really is not yours but His, He has you there to execute a plan. It is not your plan but His. If you grasp that then your next charge is to seek Him on the plan, strategy, steps, and timeline.

To Father Abraham, God made a promise of a land that he would inherit. It would be a land that he himself would not get to, neither Isaac, nor Jacob nor Moses. However, Moses would take them to the place where he would then pass the baton to Joshua who would then take Israel across the Jordan into the land they would possess.

I mention this story because what is interesting about the God we serve is that when He promises you something, it does not matter what it looks like in its current state, the word of God WILL stand. If God said, "The dead man is asleep," then to us he is dead but to God, he is asleep. Ask Jesus at the tomb of Lazarus. Jesus commanded Lazarus to come forward and guess what, after four days of being dead, the dead man came walking out of the tomb. If God said He is going to give you the land, trust that it does not matter the opposition that is before you, He has given you the land. Ask Joshua, the land he promised Abraham for his seed, he told Joshua in Chapter 1:3, that everywhere the sole of his feet touched, he had given him the land. Now for us, it seems like an incredible task. There is a truth, Joshua would have to fight some people in the process of taking the land. However, he was not fighting a losing battle. God had already given him the land so the people in the land were resisting the eviction notice; one that would have to be forcefully enforced. Praise God! There are people in your land that God will be forcefully removing. Your charge is to remember that your battle is not yours, it belongs to the Lord and He is demanding of you to trust the process.

Walking in the authority of God is walking the confident assurance that what God said He would do, He will do. It is walking and trusting even when it appears that the world is caving in on you. The storm is not sent to destroy you but to position you. Do not run from the storm, run through it. Authority is your ability to understand your truth and be firmly grounded in the promise that it possesses. Jesus said all authority was given to Him, so for me and for all of us, that means that we who are children of God, we are heirs to the authority that Jesus has received. We then need to not wheel it around carelessly but walk in boldness knowing that the One who gave it to us is the One operating through us. When we receive a word, let us wait for the plan and strategy to proceed. I can't help but remember that God not only told Joshua to go and possess the land, God also gave him the steps on how to move from one side of the Jordan to the other, how to prepare themselves, when to strike and how. When Jesus released the disciples, He told them where to go, what to do, how to respond in times of rejection and how to leave. In other words, let your discipleship plan be framed around the leading of the administrator of the mind of God, the Holy Spirit. Let your executed plan mirror the plan delivered.

You are probably ready now to take the land. Let me caution you, your next steps will be the most crucial as you move closer to employing the level of authority God has given you. Let me explain. Your authority in the place God has assigned you is greater than that same authority in an environment He did not send you. If God has sent me to minister to educators because I have a background in education and I can relate to them but instead, I go to a mechanics shop because I feel they best need the word. Guess what, I will not be flowing in my anointing. Yes, God can use me there and maybe win a few souls for the Kingdom. Guess what? I will win hundreds if not thousands of souls ministering to educators because that was my assignment. Is God glorified either way? Absolutely! However, I was not walking in obedience but in disobedience so the full plan of God for my life was not being manifested. The degree of the executed authority of God within me was limited due to my disobedience. Not only that, when we consider spiritual warfare, the enemy knows that God is a God of order so when you are walking out of order, out of alignment with God, you are rendered powerless in areas where being in the will of God, you could conquer. Ask Joshua, after destroying Jericho, the next city was Ai. This should have been an easy defeat but because there was sin in the camp, Israel was destroyed, and Joshua turned to God in disbelief. What do you do when you believe you have a sure thing but because of something that is hidden you lose or worst, face destruction? Your God given authority is contingent on total obedience to the word of God, not by one but by all that is in your camp.

The camp is important to consider. The leader receives the vision, but it is important that all who are in the camp follow to the letter the plan that has been set forth. Partial obedience is total disobedience. Authority, God given authority requires TOTAL obedience. God is looking for a people who are willing and ready to take the territory under His command. I do believe that is part of the problem with evangelism. One is the strategy of just handing out information which, may have some effect but if we think of it, Jesus never handed out a tract. Jesus never instructed His disciples nor us to hand out tracts. Yes, many have been convicted and won to the kingdom as a result of tracts but think about it, how much more would be won to the kingdom by the spoken word? How much more would be won to the kingdom by the lived word? We can ask the late greats of our time, Billy Graham, Reinhardt Bonnke, Yonge Cho, John Welsly and the list goes on. I am sure they gave out written materials, but most importantly was the fact that the millions they won to Christ were won under the spoken word in the designated location that would bring conviction and salvation of the heart. What I am saying, this day and age is looking for more people who will willfully rise and speak with boldness, authority and conviction of the Word of God in the land they have been given.

As we move forward, I want us to consider some key points that the Lord place in my spirit, import steps toward exercising your God given authority. By now you should understand that if God has given you the land, territory; the territory will only yield to you when you command it to. What is the plan? What strategies will you employ? What steps will you take? What is the timeline for you to accomplish the plan?

Plan

What is His plan? Make sure it is His plan and not your own. You want to flee the need to be in the center and let God lead. Habakkuk reminds us to write down the vision and make it plain. The vision is the plan. It is what God has shown you whether in a dream, vision, or prophecy. It is something that when you saw it you could almost touch it yet it was so far off you knew it was not in the season you are in but what was on its way. So, it is important that when these things happen, when He shows you something, find a moment to record it. That over time will evolve into the plan you will follow. By the way, when you do this, you are acknowledging that God has spoken, and it becomes your measuring stick towards attaining your goal.

Why does He assign you to that community, region or nation? No one can ever be certain as to why God has assigned you to the area you have been assigned to. As God, He not only is your creator, He also knows all about you. Every design of you has been intentionally done. Your assignment was in the works the moment you became a thought. In a time when babies were being killed at birth if they were male, God allowed Moses to not only be born but to also be position in the presence of Pharaoh's daughter so that he could grow in a school of preparation for the real assignment of his calling. If God chose you, everything you went through, every pain you suffered, every mistake you made were part of the curriculum of your preparation towards your destiny.

Why did He choose you? Always remember, Jesus had A LOT of people that surrounded Him. There were people who followed Him, wanting to hear what He had to say, see what He could do and even they themselves participate in the works of His hands. Many of them in the end said, "Crucify him," while others went away silently. Yet, He chose 12, twelve disciples were chosen to sit with Him at the table. These men would be the recipients of every word of life that would drop from His mouth. To them He would take into the annals of comprehension and revelation as to who He really was, the purpose of His coming and the charge that would be upon them in His departure. Jesus did not choose a one He could not trust to carry out the mandate before them. We know what Judas did, but if you think of it, He could trust Judas to betray Him and the only way to betray Him was by putting Him at the table. God chose you for a purpose that only you can fulfill. Don't question the call, understand the call so you can fulfill your purpose.

What are the skills you have and what are you lacking in order to execute the plan?

Now this is the tough part. To really execute the plan you have before you, you must be honest with yourself. You will need to do a thorough inventory of what skills you really have, not what you kinda have. You must be honest about what skills you are lacking so that you know how to clearly execute the plan that is before you. There is no greater leader except for the one who is transparent enough to know what they have, what they are lacking and what they need or who they need to fulfill the purpose set before them. This is how you understand who should be on your team. Your transparency will provoke a willingness to work with others greater than you can understand, yet willing to surrender to your leadership with you being the one with the vision.

Strategy

God is the chief strategist, His ways do not always make sense, but they always guarantee results. If God has given you a plan, He has the strategy. Remember, King Solomon, the wisest man to ever live wrote in Ecclesiastes that there is nothing new under the sun. What we are now undertaking in another time, looked a certain way and was effective. Now, in this age, how should it look? How can we make an old language speak to a new audience? We must keep in mind that since the strategy was not original, it came from someone, then we must constantly seek His face for our next step.

Steps

What steps are pivotal in executing the plan as you employ the strategy?

- Prayer – What prayer model, models will you engage in? Will your prayer model be individual or corporate? You could do one, the other or both. Remember always in the things of the Lord, prayer must precede and proceed the plan.

- Plan – What did He tell you to write down? Did you write down what He told you or was it your ideas as you saw fit? Remember, you are executing His plan, not yours.

- Participation – Who will you engage in this process? Note: Everyone involved in this level of work needs to be on the same spiritual page. What do I mean by that? Remember I spoke about the two kings and that only one can rule at a time. Well, if you have ten people and five have one king and the other have another king ruling their hearts then your work is already divided and doomed for failure. A thing that is divine must be divinely driven.

- Presentation – When will you roll out the plan, strategy, and participation?

- Local – Local rollout means the time spent to get all the stakeholders on the same spiritual page, sharing in the same vision. Don't be deceived, a simple yes does not seal it for everyone. You as the leader must spend time before God to know that the terrain is established so that when you bring it to the team, they are ready to go. The power and authority of God is not an appetite that you satisfy by hungry people wanting to see something awesome occur before them. No, my friends, the power of God is much more than that as discussed above. It is necessary that time and care goes into the behind the scenes planning and prayers prior to you getting the, "Go ahead."

-

☐ **Testimonial**: It took my ministry several years to get to a place where it was ready to go to the next level. Walking in the spirit and under the authority of God is work, it is patience strengthened by grace. We needed time to grow up, understand who we were as a ministry and be able to clearly articulate what we stood for, not because it was memorized but because it is a part of our DNA.

o **Global** – Global rollout does not insinuate that you are getting on a plane to take territory. It is by my definition for this section, your readiness to step out from behind the four walls and into a world that is unsafe, overwhelming, and difficult to move through if you are walking in the flesh. You are stepping out saying that the Kingdom of God has come, has it? If you do not really have understanding when you step out to conquer your community, region and world, has it? You must be very certain that the Kingdom of God is within you and that you will not stop until you fulfill the commission on your life.

Timeline

What is your timeline? What did God tell you? How long to plan? How long to pray? How long to build your team? Did He tell you when to launch out? Do not make the mistakes so many churches do. Do not try to prove yourself worthy next to the next one. Remember, the church is not the building, the congregation but the individual. Your goal is to walk as the true Church, obedient to the voice of God in all ways. The devil is always looking for ways to distract and divide great men and women of God by creating competitive spirits around whose church is largest, greatest choir, etc. To accomplish that, they launch into an aggressive evangelistic outreach and fill the pews of hurting people, most of whom are never delivered and then the enemy, shifts the focus from God's original plan for that ministry to a maintenance station. Maintaining the numbers, the status quo and not the delivery of the uncompromised Word of God. God's plan is so much greater than that so be sure to have a timeline that lines up with HIS plan, not yours, not your communities, and not what others want. It must be the plan of God executed along HIS timeline.

All Authority

18 Then Jesus came to them and said, "All authority in heaven and on earth has been given to me. 19 Therefore go and make disciples of all nations, baptizing them in the name of the Father and of the Son and of the Holy Spirit, 20 and teaching them to obey everything I have commanded you. And surely, I am with you always, to the very end of the age."

Matthew 28:18-20 (NIV)

Authority given to the church was done in a very strategic manner. Jesus walked with the disciples for three years. He walked in the spirit and taught them how to walk in the spirit. He fought and won all the battles they would ever face to ensure they would know that regardless the battle that would go before them, they did not need to fear. All they had to do, in Jesus name, was remind the adversary that he was already defeated. Jesus had prayer, plan, participation, presentation and timeline.

He tells the disciples after His mission was complete. After His crucifixion, after His resurrection and before His ascension back to His throne, He took time to let them know that everything He did here on earth was designed to position them for success. He did not tell them they would not face great trials, what He told them was that they now had all the authority they would need to face the journey ahead. If we dig deeper into the text, we will understand that it also means that all the resources that were at His disposal are now at our disposal. Why is this hard for the church to understand? Is the church in a frame of mind that there is or must be someone to whom they must bow so as opposed to looking at themselves as governing agents within a society of agencies they gravitate towards a position of submission? By submission I mean, has the church, the conveyor of all divine authority through Christ relegated its power to manmade institutions that do not even fear God, behind the scenes manipulated by the adversary? A person with authority cannot lose authority unless they give it away by succumbing to one who may not necessarily be greater than them but more cunning than they are. Let us talk with Adam, he was given all authority on earth. He lost it to one who was not greater than him but who was cunning. He slept on the job while being awake. His willfulness to eat the fruit was not because the woman invited him to but because he did not stick to the plan before him. So, authority once gained cannot be lost until you surrender it. The church is the most powerful institution established following the departure of Christ. It is the body of Christ with the power of Christ.

In sum, the authority bestowed upon the body of Christ is not to run around throwing power for all to see and to scare off the adversary. Nor is it intended to make men great so that everyone could be in awe of them. The authority of the church is to rise and be that institution that networks with the souls of all nations regardless the color, creed, social status, economic status of political affiliation. It is to be the safe haven for justice and truth at the center of which is the unadulterated word of God. It is to be the place where mentorship, leadership and governance flow from, not to destroy the minds and hearts of humanity but to restore them to the original intent of God, intimacy between The creator and His creation. If the church is going to win souls for the kingdom of God, it must break away from the religious mindset that conflict with the word of God and return to the intent of the word. Where there is love, hate cannot prevail. The church must return to LOVE, not competition, LOVE, not phobias and complexes of which denomination is better than the other, but LOVE. With LOVE, the love of God, the authority of God has its place to operate.

PAUSE: Before moving on, go to your workbook and complete the corresponding reflection for this chapter.

Apostle, Dr. Terika Smith

CHAPTER 6

Let EVA work for you

This is where we put it all together. It is one thing to read about and process Evangelism, Vicinity and Authority within the context I have described. I tell you this, it was hard for me as well. To look at my ministry and where we were, knowing that there are so many areas that God is working on in us as a team, this idea of EVA was eye opening.

We are a ministry that believes in transparency so that was not the challenge. The challenge was in understanding exactly how to do each of these things at the same time knowing we are still in a place of growth. My ministry is in its sixth year. That is a short period of time. Many churches with this length of time would have been on the streets, marking territory and putting their names out in the community in such a way that everyone would know they were there. Do not misunderstand, we have done a tiny bit of promotion and activities to let people know we are here but not intentionally. Not with the mindset described in this book. God put us in a season of preparation and discipleship, developing a strong leadership base first. We believed from the beginning that we needed workers before the harvest arrived. As stated in Luke 10:2 NKJV

"Then He said to them, "The harvest truly is great, but the laborers are few; therefore pray the Lord of the harvest to send out laborers into His harvest.

We spent time and resources working on the workers. In every ministry, we worked on the workers. God was gracious towards us, in the process of this intentional focus, God has been sending the harvest. Our congregation has steadily been growing to a point now where we have separate children's church and separate youth church on Sundays. They do their own worship, service, altar calls and plan of salvation. That is just a bit of what God has done with us. Now with this plan of EVA, we are poised to look at the land the Lord has given us and strategically proceed as He leads.

EVA will work for you when you follow the steps laid out. If there is not plan and your only goal is to have a large church, you may hurt more people than churches with a plan. In other words, it is inevitable that no church is perfect, and people may find offence wherever they go, however, when there is a system in place, there is a plan on what to do when the offense happens.

EVA will work for you if you are bold enough to step out into the land the Lord has given you even if you feel inadequate. Inadequacy brought on by man or feelings of emotions that are not of God does not dictate your ability to fail or succeed. Remember, if God said go, just go. If He says He has given you the land, even if you feel inadequate, hold on to the word that was released. God is only incapable of rejecting an unrepentant heart. He is not capable of failing. If He has spoken, it is established. He has already positioned men, women, business, systems to walk alongside you. They are just waiting for you to step.

EVA will work for you if you consider Whose authority you are carrying. It is not by your might nor by your power you are walking in but the power of the Lord. Remember, you serve the almighty, your ministry belongs to Him, your gifting belongs to Him and everything you do is centered around Him. He has the full power to fully execute everything He has told you to do. God never tells someone to do something and then abandons them. You cannot see Him, but He is always there. Walk humbly in this authority as you carry the huge responsibility given by Him.

PAUSE: Before moving on, go to your workbooks and complete the corresponding reflection for this chapter.

CHAPTER 7

My EVA plan for the ministry

Now that you have a better understanding of the EVA part of evangelism it is time to take hold of your ministry. Get your team together chart your plan, determine where you are currently and where you want to go using the EVA of EVAngelize Plan

NOTE: This chapter and template is only available in the companion workbook of this book. Look in the back of the book for instructions to obtain your copy.

Apostle, Dr. Terika Smith

CONCLUSION

It has been my pleasure and honor to share with you this God-inspired and tradition interrupting evangelism plan.

Yes, I know having big churches looks appealing and most pastors measure their success by the size of their church (not that there is anything wrong with having a large church) however, that should not be the focus. The focus of EVERY church should be the growth of souls that surrender their broken lives to Jesus.

The Bible has been saying Jesus' coming is near, well, 2000 years have gone by and He is not here yet, some may take that delay as a sign that He is not coming back at all. But we know better. It is His desire that no one perishes but that they have life in abundance (that is ONLY possible in Him). What am I saying, Jesus's return is eminent! The work is GREAT. We too must want what Jesus wants; more people won over for Him.

We love Him because He first loved us; many of us were fortunate enough to grow up in households where the word of God was a staple, but unfortunately NOT everyone had such a blessing. It is up to us to share our testimony in the way God wants us to, in the way that will be MOST effective, and will help them see what God loves them too.

God is calling you to develop an EVA plan that WORKS. It'll work because it'll be divinely inspired. God is READY to use you, I HAD to write this book (and I said HAD To because this book put itself at the VERY top of my long and important list of ministry projects) for you. I HAD to share this plan because it is URGENT.

There is a GREAT need. People are dying in LARGE numbers. In earthquakes, Tsunamis, other natural disasters, mass murders, and disease. We MUST share the gospel knowing that we are working against the clock. Against the aggressive plan of the enemy to swindle as many people as he can out of the salvation Jesus SO freely is offering to EVERYONE that will receive it.

Let's work smarter and not harder. God's plan is easy; He has laid out the foundation, cleared the way, assigned the angels to fight on your behalf and ALL you have to do is the following:

1. Write down the EVA plan
2. Communicate it to your team
3. Execute as instructed

Once you do that, you'll see God open doors in your community (territory) that you have been trying to open on your own for FAR too long.

It is my prayer you see God work in supernatural ways in your ministry and adds the laborers that are to work alongside of you.

God bless you and may your EVA plan help you fulfill the will of the Father for your ministry.

Dr. Apostle, Terika Smith

EVAngelize

WHERE TO GET YOUR EVANGELIZE WORKBOOK?

You can obtain your EVAngelize workbook and Dr. Smith's books and resources by visiting The TMS Store here: http://bit.ly/tsmstore

About The Author

Dr. Terika Smith is the President, Founder of Terika Smith Ministries and President/Pastor of Flowing Rivers International Church located in Lawrence, MA. She is the author of Except the Lord: When God Became the Builder and Write the Vision, Make it Plain Books. A lifelong educator at heart, she served for over 20 years in the field of education holding positions ranging from classroom teacher, where she taught Spanish, track and field coach, athletic director, high school principal, college professor and State of MA consultant among others. Following her love of the Lord, she left secular education to serve full time as Pastor of the Lawrence Evangelical Church. From there, she served the local community of Lawrence in ministry. During her tenure as pastor and prior to the founding of the church she currently pastors, Dr. Smith funded the institute, Send Me Minister in Training which is now partnered with IBAD in Brazil making it an international institute preparing men and women of all ages in the Word of God.

Her personal hat reveals her as mother and grandmother. In 2010, her life was changed for the better, as she writes about in her book, Except the Lord: When God Became the Builder. Her daughter, Karen entered her life as a teenager; Karen is now an adult, married to a wonderful husband, Rich. Together they have three children and are building a life to impact the world.

It is no secret to those who know her that there is no stopping Dr. Smith. Her passion for people and her passion to minister the Word of God has placed her in environments that are hungry for fresh manna. When Dr. Smith steps into a pulpit or a classroom, her constant prayer to God is for fresh manna for the people she stands before. One of her constant gratitude to God is that she may repeat a text but never a message. Her philosophy here is that, "EVERYONE needs a word relevant to them, timely to meet THEIR needs."

She has ministered in parts of the US, Dominican Republic, Cuba, Brazil, Zambia, Africa, Guatemala, and Puerto Rico. As the Lord has used her, thousands of lives have been transformed as she moves in the prophetic word leading to healings and deliverances from spiritual bondages. Her passion grows more every day knowing that if she can bring to others what God brought to her it can also change the lives of many around the world.

Dr. Smith's passion for people can also be seen in her humanitarian work. Her history records her services in Mexico where she helped countless orphans who resided in an orphanage as well as infants with cleft palates. In Africa her along with her ministry supported the schooling of children in Mombasa, Kenya and most recently, Zambia, Africa. In moments of disaster, her and her team have risen to provide relief to countless families in her local community, Puerto Rico, Guatemala and Brazil.

How to connect with Dr. Smith on Social Media:

https://www.facebook.com/TerikaSmithMinistries/

http://tsmfortheworld.org/

https://www.instagram.com/terikasmithministries/

Other Books By Dr. Terika Smith

Except the Lord: When God Became the Builder

Excepto el Senor: Cuando Dios Se Convirtió en el Constructor

My God, Our Plan: Six Key Areas to Leverage and Manage Your Life Well

Mi Dios, Nuestro Plan: Seis Areas Clave Para Aprovechar Y Administrar Bien Su Vida

Meu Deus, nosso plano: Seis Áreas-Chave para Alavancar e Gerenciar Bem Sua Vida

NOTES

Apostle, Dr. Terika Smith

EVAngelize

Apostle, Dr. Terika Smith

EVAngelize

www.ingramcontent.com/pod-product-compliance
Lightning Source LLC
Chambersburg PA
CBHW070917160426
43193CB00011B/1496